AN INTERDISCIPLINARY APPROACH TO IMPLEMENTING COMPETENCY BASED EDUCATION IN HIGHER EDUCATION

AN INTERDISCIPLINARY APPROACH TO IMPLEMENTING COMPETENCY BASED EDUCATION IN HIGHER EDUCATION

Barbara Goodman
Darren Henderson
Eileen Stenzel

The Edwin Mellen Press
Lewiston•Queenston•Lampeter

06-0084

Library of Congress Cataloging-in-Publication Data

Goodman, Barbara.
  An interdisciplinary approach to implementing competency based education in higher
education / Barbara Goodman, Darren Henderson, Eileen Stenzel.
   ·   p. cm.
  Includes bibliographical references and index.
  ISBN-13: 978-0-7734-5831-4
  ISBN-10: 0-7734-5831-X
  1. Competency-based education. 2. Education, Higher. I. Henderson, Darren. II.
Stenzel, Eileen. III. Title.

  LC1031.G66 2006
  378.1'7--dc22

                                                                    2006044967

hors série.

A CIP catalog record for this book is available from the British Library.

Author photos by Martin Martinez

Copyright © 2006 Barbara Goodman, Darren Henderson, Eileen Stenzel

The Edwin Mellen Press
Box 450
Lewiston, New York
USA 14092-0450

The Edwin Mellen Press
Box 67
Queenston, Ontario
CANADA L0S 1L0

The Edwin Mellen Press, Ltd.
Lampeter, Ceredigion, Wales
UNITED KINGDOM SA48 8LT

Printed in the United States of America

Dedication

B. G. – To my parents Betty and Livy, for encouraging my dreams and to my husband, Lee, and son, Billy, for helping to bring those dreams to fruition.

D. H. – To my mother, Barbara, for the love and support that gave me the freedom to become the person that I am today.

E. S. – To my parents, Fred and Rose, for nurturing a sense of the possible and to my husband, George and daughter, Anna, for the sustenance to persevere.

Table of Contents

Foreword

Elaine Kisisel

As a Northwestern student in the late 50s, I tried to enroll in McGovern's political science class, did my homework in Deering Library, met friends at the Rock, wore Jantzen outfits, knew the sorority secret handshake, and went to Cooley's Cupboard for milkshakes. My courses were prescribed, and my career options were limited. I listened to renowned professors speak in large lecture halls, experienced difficulties in contacting these professors, and had to rely on teaching assistants for discussions about a static curriculum. Graduation was an end in itself. Some of us continued with careers or graduate studies, others entered the world of family life.

During the late 60s, I entered the world on the other side of the lectern: teaching and conducting research. Working with students and faculties both here and abroad, I presented content-focused lessons to motivate students in their understanding of specific discipline basics for clinical applications. Lessons were sequenced and prescribed according to the development of the content and the initial levels of Bloom's Taxonomy -- knowledge, understanding and application. Underlying any curriculum development process was the assumption that students were from a homogenous pool of recent high school graduates. Student inquiries were predictable and responses were designed to support the content presented.

Beginning in the late 1980s, this approach was gradually seen as being universally problematic. Students were not homogeneous, and their diversity in learning styles and academic backgrounds were recognized and considered in designing the teaching-learning process. The role of higher education then shifted in purpose and focus. Post-secondary education became accessible to more students, causing faculties to service students, not only growing in numbers, but also blossoming from a variety of backgrounds and situations. Students were now wearing flip-flops and baseball caps, using laptops, working or raising families while in school, choosing careers from a broader selection and delaying graduation with off campus experiences. With these new challenges, higher education had to broaden its scope, incorporating the learner into the process of teaching. The eye of the educator now turned away from the blackboard and into the classroom to see the community of learners seated there. The stage was set for the development of Competency Based Education (CBE) as an effective approach to curriculum.

As illustrated in this book, CBE is based on behavioristic and holistic approaches. These views support academic growth and professional skill development with an undercurrent of increased social understanding and self-development. Beginning with an assessment of the students' academic skills and knowledge of content, faculty constructs desirable student competencies to serve as the framework for the course content and selection of the best practices from pedagogy. The relationship between faculty and student is also transformed with the student assuming an active role in the teaching-learning process. Thus, a respect for both learner and content evolves.

To learn more about this new educational environment, we are introduced to the classrooms of Eileen Stenzel, Barbara Goodman and Darren Henderson, three outstanding practitioners of this exciting approach to higher education. Although they come from diverse backgrounds, they are united in their commitment to CBE as a dynamic, interactive and reflective teaching-learning process. For each of their classrooms, competencies have been developed for both content mastery and reflective self-growth. For example, in the English classroom of Dr. Goodman, students are encouraged to enter the "world of unanticipated discovery" for academic growth and self- development with the implementation of CBE. In this "world of unanticipated discovery," students and instructor are active participants in the designing of the "backward curriculum" beginning with the "feedback loop." The "feedback loop" encompasses students, using formative evaluation methods, revealing what they have learned and what pedagogy was effective for them. Using this information, the instructor and students define student competencies for the course framework, and then, the means of achieving these competencies.

The integration of Competency Based Education into higher education has been shown to be beneficial to, not only the learner, but also the faculty. In this book, we are brought into the classrooms of Drs. Stenzel and Goodman and Mr. Henderson to witness their own transformations along with that of their students.

Elaine Kisisel

Professor Emeritus in Education

Calumet College of St. Joseph

Acknowledgements

We would like to acknowledge Dr. Elaine Kisisel and Dr. Catherine Marienau for their work as reviewers of this work.

We would also like to acknowledge our colleagues with whom we have and continue to work to implement competency based education within our various programs. They include, Ms. Kim Allen, Dr. Chris Buczinsky, Ms. Amy Comparon, Dr. Richard Damashek, Ms. Nita Danko, Dr. Geraldine Martin, Dr. Valerie Pennanen, Ms. Valerie Williams in the English Program, Mr. Denis Adams, Ms. Pat Bogash, Ms Liz Guzman-Arredondo, Ms. Jean Lubeckis, Ms. Kris Maynard, Ms. Greta Pall, in the Human Services Program, Mr. George Schaefer in the Computer Information Systems Program.

We would also like to acknowledge former instructors and colleagues who made a contribution to the evolution of this work, specifically Dr. Victor Namais and Dr. Donna Kustusch, O.P.

Finally, we would like to acknowledge the hundreds of students with whom we have and continue to engage on a daily basis in the joys and challenges of the teaching and learning process.

Introduction

Barbara Goodman, Darren Henderson, Eileen Stenzel

There are a lot of ways to tell a story. This book is one of them. The story we want to tell is about how we used Competency Based Education (CBE) to engage with what we believe to be the primary mission of higher education: to promote and sustain a contract with humanity. It is a contract that is honored in the day-to-day joys and challenges of research, teaching, and service in every college and university setting across the country and beyond. Think of the authors as characters in a narrative, the dynamics of which are shaped by their interaction with their past and present academic experiences and in the conversations they have established with one another. They are bound by a shared commitment to do the very best they can as educators and scholars in a challenging professional environment. This book is an attempt to capture the drama of the engagement with those challenges and the conversations about them that have been shared over a number of years. The drama began before we met, each in our own professional beginnings, and continued as we faced the challenges of being successful with students for whom the quality of the teaching and learning experience is often life-changing, if not life-saving.

Though a small cast, each character brings a cast of thousands and a myriad of experience to the process: former teachers and students, former and current colleagues and students, successes and failure in the classroom, and a host of anticipated challenges that will demand even better efforts on the part of each of them.

Dr. Barbara Goodman, a medievalist, student of theater and lover of literature, brings three decades of engagement with her discipline as well as a wide range of secondary and post-secondary teaching experience some in international settings. Barbara has, perhaps, the most daunting task of all since the greatest resistance to CBE often comes from those whose passions run deep within the humanities and whose commitment to promoting liberal arts education through a strong General Education curriculum is fierce.[1] Yet, in countless hours of formal and informal conversations about the joys and challenges of what we do, the most remarkable thing happened. At no point did Barbara ever convey even the slightest sense that she perceived an essential incompatibility between the basic principles of CBE and the General Education Program she developed and for which she continues to bear a great deal of academic responsibility. Quite the contrary is the case. Barbara demonstrates how CBE offers valuable tools that help students carefully recognize what it is people actually do when they engage in comparative, analytical and creative learning activities that challenge students to explore the world as it was, is and might be.

It was the engineer in this cast of characters, not the English Professor or theologian and counselor, who came up with the image of the iterative model of CBE presented here and discussed in more detail in Chapter One.

---

[1] Xin Wang, "Competency-Based Education," Baylor University, Google, 29 April 2002 <http://www3.baylor.edu/~Xin_Wang/pdf/competency.pdf>

Iterative/Waterfall Model of

Competency-Based Education

Implementation[2]

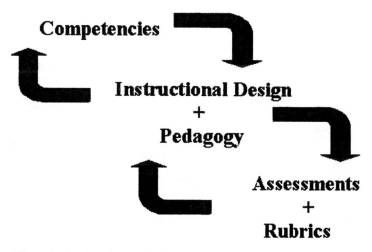

Through the iterative model, Mr. Darren Henderson, the engineer and expert in information technology, brought Zen into the conversation. Darren moves easily and creatively in a world once and sometimes still experienced as alien to the other two main characters in this story. To think sequentially, structurally and procedurally is for Darren, on the grand scale of things, just another way to ponder the wonders of the universe and, on a smaller scale, a means of staying focused on and engaged with the teaching learning process in a manner that reveres it as a life process. The iterative or waterfall model attempts to convey the "life force" of CBE sometimes lost in analysis and discussions about how to implement it. Chapter One will offer an integrate discussion of CBE, i.e. on that draws together the iterative model of a life process with a more structured analysis of the instructional design process good CBE must rely on.

---

[2] The graphic was developed by Darren Henderson to capture the dynamic of the process of implementing CBE, something that can often look more linear than we intend.

Like Barbara, Darren sees no incompatibility between CBE and his work as an educator. In Darren's view, CBE is a natural fit for an engineer and Computer Information Systems specialist. Perhaps that is the case. But Darren inserts a grasp of student-centered teaching and learning that is not always characteristic of those who teach math, science and engineering, subjects driven by the demands of mastering the equivalent of a foreign language. Often, instruction in those disciplines involves a reliance on language that is daunting and dangerous, especially for students whose orientation is more toward the arts, humanities and social sciences. Darren has helped us understand the teaching power of student-centered CBE as a means of helping students gain the initial insight into what it is they need to learn and learn how to do, insight that makes it possible for them to eventually understand and use the language of a discipline as they become more self-directing in their learning.

Dr. Eileen Stenzel is a theologian, teacher and counselor by education, training and profession. As an undergraduate student, she studied in a political science program that was known best for its Socratic approach to teaching and learning. Her "inner dialogue" as theologian has taken place within the parameters of positivistic hermeneutical methods, on the one hand, and knowledge as socially constructed and best understood in terms of its function. She studied approaches to pastoral theology and ministry that were highly catechetical in character and, at the same time, was engaged with the work of a professor who was breaking new ground in biblical and feminist scholarship, both of which challenged the positivistic and unacknowledged political underpinning of allegedly objective, value-free theology. As a counselor, she was trained in the principles of existential/humanistic approaches to clinical work but embraces a behaviorist understanding of how human beings end up where they end up. Like many college teachers, her first year in a college classroom was dismal. It was that encounter with potential failure rather than a principled embrace of CBE that marked the beginnings of the story she has to tell. The underlying principles of CBE presented in Chapter One name the tools and resources she discovered that would enable students to be successful in the classroom. Those principles became a model for understanding Competency Based Education as curricular development, instructional design and assessment that integrates all of those activities around desired outcomes.

Barbara, Darren and Eileen are both the subjects and authors of this particular narrative as a story about teaching and learning in higher education. That setting has historically placed strong value on: respect for personal and professional autonomy within the academy; uncensored inquiry and expression for which tenure is an essential resource; classroom autonomy, especially from bureaucratic intrusions; and a near sacred regard for the teaching-learning process and the primacy of the teacher-student relationship within all institutions of higher education, large and small. How CBE is perceived in relation to those core values shapes much of the debate about the appropriateness and inappropriateness of CBE for higher education.

On the one hand, there are those who promote and defend the importance of unfettered inquiry and exploration of ideas and their implications and oppose CBE, because, in their view, it threatens the very fabric of the teaching-learning activity that should prevail in colleges and universities, especially in free, democratic societies.[3] Allowing "competencies" designated by entities outside the academic system to guide the development of curriculum is, in this view, the beginning of academic sell-out to non-academic interests, especially those of the broader corporate and political world.

On the other hand, there are those whose primary activity in both undergraduate and graduate education is to prepare individuals for professional employment and advancement within a profession. "Competencies" are part of a "contract with the profession" that those who engage in professional education must be willing to enter. The success of professional education is measured, in

---

[3] Sandra Kerka, "Competency-Based Education and Training: Myths and Realities," Clearing House on Adult, Career Vocational Education (ACVE), 1998, ERIC, EBSCO, Calumet College of St. Joseph, Specker Library, 12 August 2001 <http://www.cete.org/acve/textonly/docgen.asp?tbl=mr&ID=65>; also Xin Wang.

part, by the degree to which graduates of those programs are able to function as entry-level (bachelors degree) and advanced professionals (graduate degree). The "competencies" of the profession drive the design, implementation, assessment and evaluation of these programs. In their view, if professional competencies do not include the ability to think critically and creatively, the issue is not with CBE, the issue is with the professions and the way we prepare students to enter them.

In the middle of all of this, regional accrediting agencies have sought to structure accountability for attainment of specified outcomes in higher education through an increased emphasis on assessment of student learning. The Higher Learning Commission has made assessment a central focus of its annual conferences, the self-study process and on-site visit procedures for the last decade. Accountability linked with accreditation is powerful leverage.

It is not surprising, then that the strongest support for Competency Based Education often comes from faculty engaged in professional preparation and some of the most challenging questions from faculty within traditional liberal arts areas. Professional education is driven by a need to prepare people to know and do specific things by the end of their degree. The goals of liberal arts education are often conveyed more in terms of their impact on the person of the learner than the learner as a professional-in-training. What the reader will find woven throughout this discussion is a refusal to embrace that divide. The person of the professional is an inseparable component from how that individual will do his/her job. His/her values, beliefs and attitudes, the way he or she approaches, understands and responds to the world in which he/she lives and the view of what is possible in the future world will inevitably shape the way that individual conducts him/herself as a public person.

Using the language of "competencies' is not anathema to talking about what it means to be a well-informed, world-wise, educated, reflective individual. As we will attempt to show, the language of competencies actually is critical to increasing students ability to access and benefit from the kinds of educational experiences that so enrich, expand, challenge and frustrate students out of complacency and into engagement. These educational experiences are the context in which higher education provides opportunities for students to critically examine what they have assumed to be "the case," weigh their world view against that of an emerging global perspective, encounter the culture context of human values, discover the tools of comparative ethical thinking, achieve basic mastery of quantitative and technical skills that are essential for functioning in today's world, and explore the ways in which the visual and performing arts are a medium for personal transformation and cultural enrichment. The artist takes the world in, mulls it over and conveys it back with a unique perspective and form of commentary that challenges the imagination and stirs the soul.

The three of us share with our readers the role of guardians of this contract with humanity that is the heart and soul of higher education. Rather than perpetuate suspicions about the language of "competencies," we will suggest that the language of competencies ought to include but not be limited to training within the educational experience. In this book, we have attempted to share with the reader the riches that have grown out of our efforts to honor our contract with humanity within the professional environments that have shaped and transformed our professional lives.

Though we speak for ourselves, the concerns and commitments of our colleagues are with us. We have been shaped both by their support for and their resistance to CBE. Their questions and concerns, whether pro or con, grow out of a deep and for many a life-long commitment to and involvement in higher education and its unique contract with humanity, i.e. the responsibility for nurturing and sustaining the core elements of a free society: freedom of thought and inquiry, freedom of expression, and tolerance for and appreciation of diversity. It is our hope that this volume will strengthen the conversation about educational outcomes, how to develop and how to assess them, that is of such pressing concern to most of us in higher education.

Chapter One presents CBE as the integration of observable, measurable learning outcomes with teaching and learning activities designed to help students attain those outcomes and assessment strategies that reliably measure the degree to which students are successful. The model works in a higher education setting because it requires the identification of what is involved in performing higher levels of learning and respects the core values of higher education. The proposed model does not shy away from training as a component of higher education. Neither does it assume that in the course of training students how to do things, one does not have endless opportunity to help them learn how to think critically and creatively about what they are doing and why they are doing it, as well as generate new and better ways to do it. Finally, the model we propose does not exclude student involvement in creating learning outcomes. In fact, one could write a competency-based outcome statement to encourage precisely that activity.

Chapter Two presents a discussion of implementing CBE in the Humanities. Here, Dr. Goodman will engage the reader in the interplay between the explorative, creative nature of inquiry in the humanities with the structured instructional design focus on outcomes in CBE. Here the myth that CBE values only what can be observed is counter with the argument that all learning is demonstrable regardless of the discipline in which it occurs.

Chapter Three discusses implementation within Information Technology. Darren Henderson will describe his work in developing a model of and implementing CBE within the Information Technology Program at the college. Darren makes a compelling case for the importance of a Zen-like focus on the part of an instructor and its role in driving effective assessment practices in the effort to develop technological proficiency among student of varying degrees of technical orientation

Chapter Four discusses implementation in an applied social and behavioral science program. Eileen Stenzel will describe the implementation of CBE education in Human Services, an applied social and behavioral science field. Her essays focus on the implications of CBE for strengthening clinical education. Chapter four offers a design model for developing new CBE programs as well as reviewing and revising existing programs and assessment tools used to develop program based assessment strategies as well as course-based assessment practices.

The journey we are on is rich and engaging. It originated in our experiences as students and matured in our critical reflection about those experiences using tools developed by so many who take teaching and learning seriously. It continues in the day- to-day challenges each of us faces as we meet our students for the first time and many for the third and fourth time as they complete the programs for which we are responsible. It is driven by a shared desire to do this as well as we can, for them and for the communities that will be enriched by the experiences they have with us.

Most of our students come to us living their lives as private people: moms and dads, partners, grandparents, workers, friends and neighbors. When they leave, we will have prepared most of them to assume roles as public persons: teachers, counselors, and information technology engineers, to name a few. Our embrace of CBE is, in the end, based on our experience of doing it with them. It has helped us to a better job of preparing them to engage with the issues that shape the quality of life in the communities in which they live. The success of what we do as educators is, in the end, best measured by how well they embrace their role in our shared contract with humanity.

Chapter 1

Competency-Based Education: An Evolving Model

Eileen Stenzel

Introduction: CBE and Core Values in Higher Education

Imagine the following scenario. A faculty Senate is engaged in an animated discussion of the challenges of implementing Competency Based Education (CBE) and assessment in their institution. A young member of the faculty has quietly listened to the discussion with a somewhat skeptical look on his face. Finally, after some time, he voices his concern. "It seems," he states, "that this movement toward Competency Based Education takes us back into an age of positivism, one in which the only things deemed worth knowing are those things that can be observed and measured."

This fictional but fact-based scenario captures the heart and soul of the drama that unfolds in efforts to implement CBE within higher education.[4] Those involved on both sides of the debate to implement or not implement CBE come to it with a passion for their disciplines and often an even stronger passion for the value of unfettered inquiry. They embrace values long held sacrosanct in higher education: the personal and professional autonomy of instructors and students,

---

[4] For a report of post-secondary efforts to initiate CBE in higher education see: Elizabeth A. Jones, Richard A. Voorhes and Karen Paulson, "Defining and Assessing Learning: Exploring Competency-Based Initiatives," *Report of the National Postsecondary Education Cooperative Working Group on Competency-Based Initiatives in Postsecondary Education* (Washington, D.C.: U.S. Department of Education. September 2002).

resistance to the intrusion of external bureaucracies into the classroom, and uncensored speech protected in academe unlike any other work setting.[5]

Persons who pursue careers in higher education do so, in part, because they value the learning process, the experience of engaging others in it, and the surprises that so often come at the end. The debate about the appropriateness of Competency Based Education (CBE) often seems less driven by a resistance to stating intended outcomes and more by an intense desire not to limit the process to those intended outcomes. Many voice concern that the educational process will be driven more by the specific demands of job performance and less by engagement with questions, issues, concerns, perspectives, values, conflicts and unspoken as well as spoken concerns. For them, the emergence of unintended but equally valuable outcomes in a learning process goes to the soul of the teaching-learning process.

Embedded in this debate is a desire to protect the students' opportunity to shape unanticipated outcomes. To the extent that CBE is viewed by its opponents as an attack on these time honored traditions and an attempt to put more emphasis in the experience of the teaching-learning process on intended outcomes and less on the process of attaining them and the surprises it can engender, CBE will be suspect.[6] The question posed by the young scholar, whose name is legion, is one that advocates of CBE must address in advancing models of CBE appropriate to a higher education setting. This chapter presents a detailed discussion of an iterative model of Competency Based Education that takes this young man's concerns seriously. This book is an attempt resolve them by showing how CBE can be

---

[5] Alice Bedard Voorhes, "Creating and Implementing Competency-Based Learning Models," *Measuring What Matters Competency-Based Learning Models in Higher Education,* Ed. Richard A. Voorhes, New Directions for Institutional Research 110 (San Francisco: Jossey-Bass 2001); Cf. C. Chappell, "Quality & Competency Based Education and Training," *The Literacy Equation* (Red Hill, Australia: Queensland Council for Adult Literacy, 1996)71-79 and T. Hyland, *Competence, Education and NVQs: Dissenting Perspectives* (London: Cassell, 1994).

[6] Robert V. Bullough, Jr., Robert S. Patterson, Clifford T. Mayes, "Teaching as Prophecy," *Curriculum Inquiry* 32:3 (2002); also Y. Peters Waghid, "Non-Instrumental Justification of Higher Education View Revisited: Contesting the Philosophy of Outcomes-based Education in South Africa," *Studies in Philosophy & Education* 22.3/4 (2003) 245, 2.

implemented in a manner that shows the deepest regard for teaching excellence and curriculum design that approaches undergraduate professional education as occurring best in the context of a genuinely liberal arts education that embraces the import role of information technology within those professions.

The discussion is organized around two initial challenges that any faculty and administration must be willing to face in implementing CBE. The first is the challenge of developing a model of CBE that represents *consensus* among the faculty about what CBE is and is not, especially within a higher education setting. The strongest barrier to consensus is usually the failure to address and resolve faculty concerns about CBE especially its origins in vocational education and training programs and view them, instead, as the reactions of out of touch, uninformed faculty.[7] The second challenge is to develop planning and implementation protocols that can guide program-based implementation with an acknowledged and valued commitment to a broad range of learning outcomes. In this model, the one insistence the reader will encounter is that the more educators can say what they mean by "critical thinking", the ability to synthesize, the ability to think creatively, the ability to problem solve and the difference between knowledge as information and summary as the demonstration of initial insight, the mores students will be able to achieve those desired ends. In other words, we reject the notion that specifying outcomes is a new venture in higher education. Higher education has always involved attainment of outcomes. What is new is the emphasis on specifying those outcomes in demonstrable ways as both an instructional and assessment tool.

CBE makes all the rules of learning public. CBE assumes that teaching involves teaching students how to learn, not just what to learn. CBE assumes that in the end what matters most is not what we said we wanted are student to be able to do. What matters is what they can demonstrate. What matters most is

---

7 For an excellent presentation of CBE as a training model see: Rick Sullivan, "The Competency-Based Approach to Training," RePro Line The Reading Room JHPIEGO Strategy Paper September 1995, Google, 6 July 2005
<http://www.reproline.jhu.edu/english/6read/6training/cbt/cbt.htm#CBT>.

what they can take with them as they assume the role of public persons living enriched private lives.

Beginning Where We Ended

The authors of this text entered into a process of implementing Competency Based Education from a variety of starting points. We had the shared experience of our institution's long been involved in CBE as demonstrated by our Life Experience Assessment Portfolio (LEAP) Program. We have all had opportunities to serve as reviewers of those portfolios. In the LEAP program, students have an opportunity to demonstrate the knowledge and skills they have acquired in prior professional experience, paid or unpaid. This approach to CBE is among the most long-standing in higher education and correlates with the beginning of accelerated undergraduate degree programs. It has and continues to challenge the "units of credit" model of measuring student learning insisting that neither credit hours alone nor grades alone convey what in fact it is that students have learned in a course and in a program of study.

The institutional experience of crediting learning that occurred outside the confines of academe has and will continue to have its detractors. The process of implementing those types of CBE programs will continue to face the challenge of developing assessment standards that are fair and uniform, to the extent that they can be. While that is not the model that we are working from it is the model that helped institutions shaped what we term a holistic, pedagogical approach to Competency Based Education. That is to say, we recognize that a student's experience is best conceived as an integrated whole. Our appeal to professional education in a liberal arts education is intended to convey this holistic orientation. A student's ability to transfer knowledge and skill beyond the classroom in which those skills were first acquired demands an integration of opportunities represented by initiatives like writing-across-the-curriculum which has been going on for decades.

The reader will encounter this shared pedagogical commitment throughout these various essays. Each of us acknowledges our student-day experiences of "teaching-centered" classrooms in which the focus was on what the student was able to do with what the teacher gave them. Each of us recognizes that in our earliest days of teaching we had the tendency, to varying degrees, to duplicate this model. Each of us gives an accounting of the challenge of implementing Competency Based Education as one that forced us to concentrate on the behaviors of both teaching and learning in a more disciplined, focused, student-centered manner than any of us had prior to starting this project. The following graphic conveys that experiences.

Iterative/Waterfall Model of
Competency-Based Education

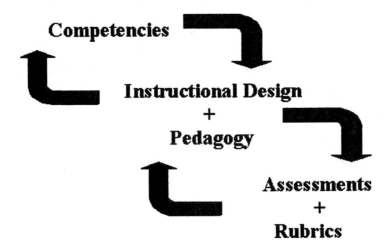

Competencies

Instructional Design
+
Pedagogy

Assessments
+
Rubrics

This iterative model of CBE proposed in this chapter evolved from the challenges faced in college classrooms, discussions with colleagues and the desire to achieve teaching excellence. In other words, the model was not the starting point for getting into CBE. Rather, it is now a way of naming and describing what evolved out of a process of engagement with the challenges, frustration, failures and successes in the teaching-learning process. It represents the product of collective efforts to personally teach well and collectively engage in the responsibility for the curriculum which rests most heavily with a college faculty. Curriculum and instruction is our job more than it is anyone else's job in a college or university setting.

The model is the product of years of efforts to overcome some of the worst mistakes that many experience as students and duplicate as teachers. This particular effort reflects the authors' experiences of meeting these challenges over decades. The tool most helpful in that process and a cornerstone of the model of

CBE proposed here is, *Bloom's Taxonomy of Educational Objectives* (The Taxonomy).[8]

The Taxonomy "works" for two reasons. First, it provides faculty with a tool that discusses attainment of educational goals they deeply value yet challenges them to think of those goals as attained sequentially. The Taxonomy gives a shared language for talking about the process by which student move toward higher levels of learning. That, in turn, provides instructors with a framework for thinking about how their actions as teachers influence that process.

Second, the Taxonomy "works" because it is the prevailing context in which CBE is discussed in the broader national and international discussions about CBE in higher education.[9] For these reasons, the model of CBE presented here relies heavily but not exclusively on Bloom's Taxonomy of Educational Objectives.[10]

Section One discusses an evolving model of CBE within a discussion of some of the unique problems encountered in the attempt to implement CBE in a higher education setting. Section Two presents a model for designing new CBE programs as well as reviewing and revising existing programs. The model demonstrates how a "backward design/forward implementation" process can guide those processes.

---

[8] Benjamin S. Bloom (ed).*Taxonomy of Educational Objectives. Handbook I: Cognitive Domain* (New York: McKay, 1956); Benjamin S. Bloom (ed), *Taxonomy of Educational Objectives. Handbook II: Affective Domain* (New York: McKay, 1973).

[9] Alice Bedard Voorhes; Steven G. Weinrach and Kenneth R. Thomas, " A Critical Analysis of the Multicultural Counseling Competencies: Implications for the Practice of Mental Health Counseling". *Journal of Mental Health Counseling* 24.1 (2002) 20-35. This article contains an excellent summary of the history of Competency-Based Education.

[10] In addition to Bloom's Taxonomy the work of Robert Gagne indirectly influenced this effort to establish a shared model of CBE and attempt to implement it. Cf. Robert Gagne, *The Conditions of Learning* (New York: Holt, Rinehart andWinston, 1985). Gagne's work is important because he focused the types of learning tasks associated with various levels of learning and the corresponding types of instructional activities that enhances student's engagement in theses tasks and mastery of the objectives.

Section One: Competency-Based Education: A Working Model

Competency-Based Education (CBE): A synthesis of two approaches

Two models of Competency Based Education shape the international discussion about CBE and its implications for higher education.[11] The first model identifies competencies as those knowledge and skill sets needed for a particular profession. The preparatory curriculum is designed around the development of those specific work-related competencies. This contribution of this model to the discussion of implementing CBE in a higher education setting is its requirement of a backward design/forward implementation of curriculum. That is, curriculum design begins with a clearly defined set of outcomes the student will need to be well-prepared to function in a professional setting and/or post-baccalaureate educational environment and implements instruction that moves toward attainment of these outcomes.

The second model refers more generally to a process of instructional design (i.e. the formulation of objectives, the design of teaching-learning strategies and the use of assessment tools) in which behavioral objectives, teaching-learning strategies and assessment tools are strategically linked.[12] In this model, "competencies" refers to those specific observable, measurable learning outcomes intended in a unit of instruction. Attainment of these outcomes is directly related to the teaching-learning strategies students experience and the effectiveness of both formative and summative assessment strategies in measuring student attainment of theses outcomes. This second model contributes the idea of the strategic link between educational objectives, teaching-learning strategies and assessment as a key component of effective implementation of CBE.

---

[11] Sandra Kerka,

[12] Cf. Gagne. Students and faculty alike have found this image of linked objectives, teaching strategies and assessment especially helpful in both formal and informal discussions about CBE. Of particular interest to some was the notion that behavioral objectives, teaching-learning strategies and assessment can best be perceived in a more circular than linear relationship to one another.

**Competency-Based Education (CBE): Developing A Model in
Response to Issues Related to Its Origins**

1. The issue of "training" vs. "education"

CBE originated in industrial settings where effective training is critical to
quality control, safety and efficient management of fiscal and human resources to
ensure the highest possible return on investment.[13] The desired training outcomes
were those identified in empirical studies to be most related to several key types
of workplace needs: improved quality of the product or service, greater efficiency
in the use of resources, improvement in the return on investment, improved
safety.[14] These outcomes, coupled with the need to reinforce the transfer of basic
knowledge and skills to the workplace, guide the design and delivery of training
modules. The most serious reservation about the implementation of CBE in a
higher education setting is its origins in training programs. Higher education
understands itself to be about more than training, where training is seen as the
performance of motor skills and/or rote-acquired behaviors separate from
engagement of higher order thinking. Nevertheless, these two elements of CBE,
i.e. the importance of *measurable, observable outcome statements* (i.e. objectives)
that transfer to the work place, and *assessment* as a key component of ensuring
that this transfer of knowledge and skills occurs, is an important part of what CBE
can contribute to improving the quality of learning outcomes in higher education.
Of particular importance is the role assessment plays as *both* a teaching tool and a
measurement tool.

In CBE assessment is *both* a formative and summative process. Formative
assessment is a tool for *improving the quality of instruction and student learning.*

---

[13] Kerka,

[14] The job-training roots of Competency-Based Education are well established. Career-oriented college curricula, especially within junior college systems, reflect this link between the demands of a job and the requirements of an educational program. Cf. Holland College: http://www.hollandc.pe.ca/CBE/Cbe.htm, Virginia Department of Education http://www.cteresource.org/VDOE/CTE/cbeindex.html, Century College http://www.century.cc.mn.us/programsdepts/departments/cbe/

It allows for immediate feedback to students while they are involved in a learning sequence. Summative assessment serves as a tool for *measuring the attainment of outcomes.* Assessment strategies that challenge students to engage with material that simulates the post graduation experience can increase the likelihood that the student will transfer his/her academic skills to the work and/or graduate school environment.

In addition to the focus on assessment, CBE challenges college educators to re-think the extent to which the importance of training in the mastery of academic skills has been overlooked or more, feared as a watering down of the academic experience. "Training" simply means learning how to do something. Higher education is and should remain committed to the development of critical thinking skills throughout the curriculum. For many, the "training origins" of CBE are perceived to minimize this commitment or eliminate it altogether. Certainly, there are approaches to CBE that engender this concern. But such does not have to be the case.

The commitment to critical thinking is, in fact, well specified by the mastery of upper level cognitive and affective learning outcomes, especially in colleges with a deep commitment to the liberal arts. This commitment can, in fact, be enhanced by an acceptance of a well thought out training component in instructional design. Higher order thinking skills are acquired through modeling, demonstration, practice and critique. CBE education can enhance rather than diminish attention to the mastery of higher level learning by insisting that: 1) learning objectives state these outcomes is observable measurable terms; 2) instruction is designed around direct teaching for attainment of these outcomes; and 3) assessment drives the process.

2. The issue of intended vs. unintended outcomes

College instructors tend to reflect two types of ideological commitment to the teaching-learning process. On the one hand, there are those who subscribe to the view that a professor's job is to create an experience for the student. The attained outcomes are the product of whatever the student does with that experience. That outcome may be expressed in a term paper, a project, and/or a collection of test scores. In assessment, what is measured is what the student did with what the experience the professor provided. The expectation of the "college-ready" student is that he/she comes prepared to create those products.

On the other hand, there are those who subscribe to a more structured and deliberate approach to instructional design. Here one usually finds individuals with formal training educational theory and practice and/or those who are engaged in undergraduate and graduate professional education and training. While diverse philosophies and approaches to teaching and learning prevail, there is some consensus among this second group. They agree that:

1. the curriculum offered to students must prepare them for existing professional and emerging challenges;

2. learning outcomes are directly related to *the quality of instruction* faculty provide making teachers responsible for student outcomes;

3. good teaching must take into account diverse learning styles;

4. assessment drives the learning process, i.e. learning begins with assessment, is guided by assessment and is measured by assessment.

Implementing CBE in higher education must take into account and be prepared to address the concerns of the faculty as a body into account. These can be summarized as follows. CBE is perceived by many to:

1. collapse education and training;

2. limit the scope and appeal of the educational experience to intended outcomes at the expense of attention to the unintended outcomes that students generate; and, most seriously of all; and,

3. favor a more narrow professional preparation over the importance of broad, general knowledge.

The question is whether Competency Based Education has applicability within a broad liberal arts curriculum all of which is not directly focused on professional preparation. The model proposed here, is that these concerns about its limits have less to do with the underlying principles of Competency Based Education and more to do with perceiving it solely in terms of particular types of learning outcomes that reflect certain types of professional preparation curricula. Mastering the ability to consistently offer empathic responses to counseling clients is a measurable and observable learning outcomes. So it critical thinking. In both, one simply needs to know what oral and /or written behaviors demonstrate the skill. The issue is not really about Competency-Based Education. The issue is whether or not one agrees that all educational outcomes can be specified in observable measurable terms. The principles of Competency-Based Education suggest that they can.

Building the Bridge To Common Concerns

In CBE, 'outcomes' refer to clearly stated, *behavioral, (i.e. observable and measurable), objectives.*[15] CBE is a structured focus on the activities of teaching and learning that define the process by which students master those outcomes.[16] Instructional design is simply the process of identifying activities that will be used to achieve that goal. That process includes three things instructors have and will continue to do in college and university classrooms. Instructors will do things, i.e. engage in teaching activities, that they believe will help students learn. Instructors will ask students to do things, i.e. engage in learning activities, that they believe will enhance students' learning. And instructors will assess how well students have developed the knowledge, skills and/or attitudes that define the content of a course.

---

[15] Lynne Tomasa, "Strategy to Implement Competency-Based Education," ACGME Outcomes Project Educational Outcomes Group, Google, 1 September 2005 <www.ahsc.arizona.edu/azmec/ Strategy%20to%20Implement%20Competency%20Based%20Education.pdf>.

[16] Jones, Voorhes and Paulson. CBE is presented as the bridge between the use of credit hours as a way of measuring student learning and the demand for more direct demonstrations of student learning.

CBE puts language, structure and focus to this process. It most fundamental underlying principle is that there is a link between learning outcomes and teaching-learning activities. CBE uses concrete rather than abstract terms to talk about learning outcomes. CBE relates teaching activities to the variety of ways in which people learn. Finally, CBE relies heavily on formative assessment as a teaching tool in addition to summative assessment as a tool of final evaluation.

The goal of formative assessment is to improve individual student's attainment of learning outcomes and increase the number of students who master these goals. The task is to identify what is and is not working and adjust teaching and/or learning activities to improve student performance. Summative assessment, on the other hand, refers to the process of measuring the degree to which students have mastered the stated objectives by the end of any given instructional unit (i.e. class, course, or program). Summative assessment may produce data that has implications for the process of learning but the changes will impact students in the future. Formative assessment supports change while a course or other educational or training activity is in progress. Summative assessment improves the next starting point.

The basic premise of CBE as stated above is that there is a direct link between attainment of learning outcomes and teaching-learning activities. That premise rests on four *basic assumptions* that characterize CBE.

1. The likelihood that students will master the desired outcomes is improved when those outcomes are clearly stated in **measurable, observable terms and presented at the outset** of instruction.

2. The attainment of student outcomes is **directly related to** the design and delivery of instruction and effective assessment.

3. The effective **transfer of knowledge, skills and attitudes** to non-academic settings, i.e. the workplace can be enhanced by instructional design, teaching strategies and assessment that

challenge students to apply what they have learned to work-related problems.

4.   The long-range goal of learning is to enhance students' ability to master the learning process, i.e. to strengthen their ability to function as **self-directed learners**.[17]

These assumptions about the importance of <u>and</u> relationship between behavioral objectives and the conditions under which those objectives are mastered, are the defining elements of CBE. The key to getting started at implementing CBE is knowing what it is students should know and be able to do when a unit of instruction has ended. The key that starts the process is writing clear, observable, measurable behavioral objectives. What follows is a discussion of the development of behavioral objectives as a defining element of CBE *using Bloom's Taxonomy of Educational Objectives*, hereafter referred to as, The Taxonomy.[18]

Bloom's Taxonomy of Educational Objectives as a CBE Design Tool

'Competency' refers simply to the ability to do something. CBE instructional units are designed to maximize student attainment of desired outcomes, i.e. competencies. Instruction is the process of identifying, giving information about, demonstrating, and providing supervised practice of these competencies with a focus on the transferability of academic skills to other academic and non-academic settings at all points along the way. Formative assessment provides students with meaningful feedback as they work toward mastery of the competencies. Summative assessment measures how well those

---

[17] The potential of Competency Based Education to engender a stronger commitment to the importance of life-long learning is an especially compelling feature of CBE in pre-professional and professional education programs. Fostering a commitment to life-long learning is a major responsibility of pre-professional and professional programs of education.

[18] Benjamin S. Bloom, John Thomas Hastings, *Handbook on Formative and Summative Evaluation of Student Learning* (New York: McGraw-Hill, 1971); also H. J. Klausmeier, *Educational Psychology* (New York: Harper & Row, 1985).

competencies have been mastered. To be effective both students and teachers need to be crystal clear on the desired outcomes.

Bloom's Taxonomy of Educational Objectives is a valuable tool for implementing CBE for two reasons. First, it describes distinct levels of learning in concrete, observable terms that can guide the development of behavioral objectives. These types of stated objectives enhance a teacher's ability to a) design appropriate and effective instruction, i.e. instruction that is linked directly to the desired outcomes, and b) design and implement effect assessment tools. Second, the Taxonomy sequences the learning process. This sequencing of learning outcomes can guide in the planning of teaching-learning activities that lead the student from relatively simple to more complex learning outcomes that are dependent on those earlier stages for success. What follows is a brief overview of *The Taxonomy*.

The Taxonomy identifies three areas in which learning occurs. These "learning domains" are: cognitive, affective and psychomotor. Each domain is presented as a sequential ordering of lower level to higher level learning outcomes. The ordering is 'sequential' because the attainment of higher level learning is dependent on success in the lower levels of learning. What follows is a condensed version of each domain indicating the name of each level, a brief definition of that level and verbs that represent the types of behaviors that represent each level of learning. [19]

Table 1 summarizes each of the tree domains, gives a brief definition and, in italics, verbs describing behaviors that indicate performance at each level of learning. Often proponents of CBE will talk about "operationalizing" our language". This simply means identifying the behaviors that demonstrate learning. The verb answers the question, "What is it that students can do when they 'know about' and 'understand' something, are able to apply that knowledge

---

[19]. The reader interested in viewing additional resources that speak to the application of the taxonomy to instructional design should conduct an Internet search on "Bloom's Taxonomy." A large number of colleges and universities have created websites that address the use of the taxonomy in the instructional design process.

and understanding, are able to analyze, synthesize and evaluate? The verbs are simply ways of stating these outcomes in behavioral terms.

Table 1   Bloom's Taxonomy of Educational Objectives: Cognitive and Affective Domains[20]

Cognitive Domain	Cognitive Domain Descriptors	Affective Domain	Affective Domain Descriptors
6. *Evaluation*: making judgments about the value of method and materials for a stated purpose	appraise, compare, conclude contrast, critique, defend, explain, interpret, support	5. *Internalizing*: Value system controls behavior in a consistent, predictable manner; solves problems objectively, revises judgments and changes behavior in light of new evidence	act, discriminate, display, influence, listen, modify, perform, practice, propose, qualify, question, revise, serve, solve, verify.
5. *Synthesis*: put parts together with new meaning, method and/or purpose	modify, organize, plan, rearranges, reconstruct, revise, rewrite,	4. *Organizing*: Establishes and uses value priorities to resolve value conflicts; accepts professional ethical standards; prioritizes time to meet conflicting needs.	adhere, alter, arrange, combine, compare, complete, defend, explain, formulate, generalize, identify, integrate, modify, order, organize, prepare, relate, synthesize.
4. *Analysis*: the ability to identify unstated assumptions, distinguish fact from hypothesis, and see the interrelationship among ideas	breakdown into parts, compare, contrast, deconstruct, discriminate, distinguish, illustrate, infer, relates, select,	3. *Valuing*: attaches value to an object or behavior; values diversity; is able to plan and commit to a plan of action.	complete, demonstrate, explain, follow, form, initiate, invite, join, justify, propose, report, select, share, study, work.
3. *Application*: the ability to apply ideas to concrete situations; problem-solving	Compute, construct, demonstrates, manipulate, modify, operate, predict, produce, show, solve, use	2. *Responding*: active participation, on the part of the learners; attends and reacts to a particular phenomenon.	answer, assist, aid, comply, discuss, greet, help, label, perform, practice, present, read, recite, report, select, tell, write.

[20] Adapted from: Bloom (1956; 1973), op.cit.

2. *Understanding:* ability to summarize	explain, give examples, paraphrase, summarize,	*1. Receiving*: willingness to attend; listens to others with respect.	ask, choose, describe, follow, point to, select, sit, reply, use.
1. Knowledge: the ability to recall information: learning is 'learning about'.	Define, describe, identify, know, label, list, match, name, outline, recall, recognize, reproduce, select, state		

In each domain, learning ranges from relatively simple processes to complex and innovative tasks. For example, using the Cognitive Domain learning objectives range from simple recall of information (knowledge) to creative ways of synthesizing ideas and proposing new directions for thinking about a problem, issue or topic. In the Affective Domain learning objectives range from a willingness to attend to a topic or task to the experience of the impact of learning on ones value system, what is sometimes referred to as the transformative character of higher education. In the Psychomotor Domain learning objectives start with rote repetition of a motor skill activity and extend, at the highest level, to innovative psychomotor behaviors.

The Taxonomy is a useful tool in implementing CBE for three reasons. First, it helps teachers answer the most fundamental instructional design question, "What should students know and know how to do at the end of the class, course and/or program of study?" Second, the taxonomy focuses the answer to this question on *observable, measurable outcomes* thereby helping faculty specify the behaviors that demonstrate attainment of learning outcomes. This specificity is necessary to link instructional design with valid and effective assessment strategies. Clearly stated, observable, measurable outcomes also serve to enhance students' clarity about the goals they are attempting to achieve and the criteria that will be used to assess their level of attainment. Third, stating learning objectives in behavioral terms can aid instructors in the task of designing instructional *activities* that support mastery of these learning behaviors and assessment tools that do, in fact, *measure* the extent to which these outcomes have been mastered.

A Defining Characteristic of CBE: Linking Behavioral Objective, Instructional Activity and Assessment

In CBE, behavioral objectives, teaching-learning activities and assessment drive the teaching-learning process. CBE is characterized by the way in which these three components are strategically linked to one another. This strategic "linking" is not linear but functions "in the round". Using this image, CBE offers three simple steps for designing an instructional unit. First, the instructional objective, whether abstract like "critical thinking" or concrete like "Chi Square analysis" needs to be identified in behavioral, i.e. measurable and observable terms. Second, instructional and learning activities need to be designed around these behaviors. The teaching and learning process must identify, demonstrate and provide supervised practice, with meaningful feedback, of the desired learning outcome. Third, assessment tools need to be developed that in fact actually assess desired outcomes. Over reliance on tools that assess primarily at the knowledge or understanding levels on the taxonomy undermine the attainment of higher levels of learning and the integrated level of performance that should characterize undergraduate and graduate professional education. What follows is an example of how these three steps implement CBE in the design of a counseling class session.

Step One The Behavioral Objectives

1.   Students will be able to define the counseling skill of hearing the opportunity for growth in the problem presented by the client.[21] (Cognitive Domain: Level 1).

---

[21] Cf. Gerard Egan, *The Skilled Helper* (California: Brooks/Cole, 1998; Gerard Egan, *Exercises in Helping Skills* (California: Brooks/Cole, 1998).

2.   Students will be able to explain what this skill is and how it is used to another person not in the class (Cognitive Domain: Level 2).

3.   In a role play students will be able to demonstrate the ability to reflect back to a client the strength/opportunity in the problem situation the client faces. (Cognitive Domain: Level 3)

Step Two The Teaching--Learning Activities (The number in parentheses relates the learning activity to the pertinent objective above.)

1.   Students will take part in a class discussion of the clinical ability to listen for opportunities in problem situations. (1)

2.   Students will tape record a discussion with someone not currently enrolled in this class in which the student explain what is meant by "attending", how this skill is practiced in the clinical relationship and why it is so important to effective counseling. (2)

3.   Students will observe a demonstration and follow-up explanation of the use of this skill in a simulated clinical setting. (1 and 3)

4.   Students will complete the section ""Problems and Opportunities" in the Student Manual.[22] (3)

Step 3 Assessment:

a. Formative Assessment:

1.   In class students will write a three sentence summary that explains the "listening for opportunities in problem situations" skill to a client. (2)

2.   In class students will identify the strength/opportunity they hear in a simulated clinical scenario. (2)

b. Summative Assessment:

---

[22] Egan, *Exercises in Helping Skills* 6-8.

1.   Short Quiz: Students will be able to correctly define the "listening for opportunities in problem situations" skill. (1)

2.   Case Verbatim: Students will be able to identify a strength/opportunity they hear in a verbatim exchange between a client and a counselor. (2)

3.   Case Study: Students will be able to transfer to listening for strengths/opportunities skill in their on-going clinical simulation exercise. (3)

The linking of objectives, teaching-learning activities and assessment assumes two things. First, it assumes that the transfer of knowledge and skills is not automatic; it is itself, an acquired skill. Second, the linking of the three components assumes that the skills associated with higher levels of learning (as articulated on the taxonomy) are acquired. The ways in which students can acquire these skills are rich and varied. Not the least important is the model of learning instructors demonstrate in the way they deliver their courses and interact with students. In CBE this modeling process becomes conscious and intentional. Higher order learning is a planned outcome.

Section Two: A Model for CBE Program Design and Implementation

This section offers a model for planning and developing a new competency based academic program. The model can also be used to assess and modify existing programs to ensure a stronger focus on attainment of desired outcomes.

The underlying design principle is referred to as the "backward design/forward implementation" model of curriculum development. The *first task* of competency-based program design is to construct a clear picture of desired post-degree outcomes: what it is that professionals in a given field are and will be challenged to do now and in the future? These challenges create a need for professionals who can engage with, guide and support professions that must respond to changing needs and incorporate new resources into professional practice and on-going professional development. For example, teacher education must equip students to meet the challenges of public education in the landscape of demanding urban environments and incorporate the ever-expanding resources of information technology into the delivery of instruction in both urban and rural settings. Health care professionals must be prepared to engage effectively with the flow of new information and ideas of the causes, treatment and prevention of illness and creation of healthier societies. In these as in all professions, the challenge cannot be limited to teaching students what they need to know in order to function in those professions. Rather, the emphasis must be on preparing future professionals with the foundation that will enable them to continue to learn what they need to know to meet the emerging challenges within any occupation.

One of the most effective ways to create this clear picture of the end product also serve creates one of the most controversial issues in implementing Competency Based Education: partnership with the professions. Providing opportunities for curricular development to begin with the observations and recommendations of active professionals can be perceived as redefining the educational process into extensions of corporate training centers: we teach what corporate American wants taught. No one involved in implementing Competency Based Education should minimize the danger that of academic institutions losing their ability to provide comparative, critical perspectives on how professions function in the broader society. That said, the model used to plan and develop these programs needs to reflect a serious commitment to ensuring that all education is critical education. The following model was used to design a graduate program in professional education with that type of commitment firmly embedded in the process.

Step One: "The Job": What do we know about the job as it is done now and will be done in the future? The following questions can guide this process.

1.   What do members of this profession currently do?

2.   What will members of this profession do in the future that is different from what they do now?

3.   What, if anything, are the unique challenges that members of this profession will face in the 21st Century?

4.   If there are differences between what members of this profession do now and in the future how those differences be characterized?

5.   What are the strengths of current approaches to the practice of this profession?

6.   What are the strengths of new approaches to the practice of this profession?

Step Two: The Competencies To Do the Job: What competencies, i.e. knowledge, skills and attitudes, will be required to be effective in this profession in the 21st century?

Step Three: The Education and Training Needed to Master the Competencies: How will these competencies be developed? What resources, experiences and tools are needed to develop these competencies? The goal of Competency-Based Education is to work toward mastery of clearly stated measurable learning outcomes that result in a student who can integrate the knowledge, skills and attitudes into a coherent demonstration of professional competence. The task here is to a) identify strategies for developing the knowledge base, the skill base, and the attitude/value base, and b) strategies for integrating these three elements.

A curriculum that is responsive to these kinds of planning questions will reflect both a curricular core and courses that develop specialized knowledge and skills. For example, most professional programs require a course in professional ethics. In these courses, students should be given an opportunity to master: a) the standards of professional behavior that are articulate by professional organizations; and b) the knowledge and skills they need to engage the broader issues that define the social, political and economic function of that profession. Physicians need to be able to engage with the questions of the parameters of their professional behavior and the parameters of their profession as part of the issue of how health care is delivered in the United States and elsewhere. Law enforcement personnel need to understand both the standards of behavior that guide them while on the job and the ethical issues that shape the way law enforcement should and should not function in a democratic social system. Teachers need to understand the standards of professional behavior within school systems as well as the broader social and political issues that shape debate about the future of education. In this setting students need to demonstrate increasing mastery of the ability to gather, assess and apply information to solving problems that mirror what they will encounter in the profession.

Step Three: Assessment: How will progress toward and attainment of mastery be assessed?

Step Four: Accountability: What interventions will be taken to improve progress toward attainment of mastery?

This type of process is consistent with the standards of best practice in designing CBE: it begins with assessment, it is enhanced by assessment and it ends with assessment. Done well, CBE design will end up back where it started with new insights into the same questions, new questions, and ideas about how to improve the quality of the program even before the first student has graduated. *The Taxonomy* will serve as one of several guides to ensure that the curriculum moves students beyond a knowledge base. The Taxonomy will focus specific attention on the attainment of higher levels of learning and on the need for the *integration* of the cognitive and affective domains.

The Taxonomy will also serve as a tool for the design of different types of instructional modules for different types of learning outcomes. For example, the development of a common core curriculum proceeds around clearly stated knowledge, skills and attitudes determined to be the foundation of the ability to work within a profession. Specialized knowledge and skills identify specific demands professionals in this field will face. Theses competencies shape the second part of the curriculum. Finally, the need to demonstrate students' ability to integrate general and specialized knowledge and skills with examples of real challenges they will face in the work setting can be met through carefully designed and implemented tutorials, capstone, practicum and /or internship experiences.

Conclusion

The task of implementing CBE in higher education is both challenging and frustrating. The process should begin with a careful and critical examination of CBE among the faculty before any vote was cast to implement it. Conflict avoided is often conflict intensified. The issues on both sides of the discussion are critical to effective implementation in a higher education setting. On the one hand, those who oppose CBE education do so because they view the function of higher education as far more than job preparation. They value the process of helping students develop insight into the world in which they live, the cultures that are represented in it and the history of ideas that shape our understanding of and response to it. Additionally, many feel that Competency-Based Education leaves the student out of what should be a contract for learning. It rests all decisions about outcomes in the hand of the instructor thus working against a more student-centered learning environment.

On the other hand, proponents of CBE argue that the clarification of learning outcomes that CBE requires can *only enhance* the attainment of all educational outcomes regardless of their orientation in General Education or Professional Preparation. Advocates often identify the role of critical thinking skills in both General Education and Professional Education as an example. They argue that identifying the kinds of intellectual behaviors one engages in the process of doing critical thinking increases the likelihood that students will become better able to demonstrate it and instructors will be more effective at assessing it.

Proponents of CBE often argue, as well, that CBE reflects a significant shift in the student population served by institutions of higher education. Higher education is no longer the prerogative of sons and daughters of upper middle class parents, young people with significant amounts of leisure time. Higher education, at least in American Society, is entrenched in the American value of universal access to education and is linked inextricably with career preparation and enhancement. The question is not whether CBE education should be implemented but how.

Colleges and universities can implement at three levels: course, program and institution. The experience of the authors is primarily course and program-based implementation. Institutional implementation can occur across the curriculum through the cooperative efforts of program faculty and an Office of Institutional Research and/or Assessment. Such efforts require the development and maintenance of student performance data and, in some cases, the use of formal assessment tools that will require institutional fiscal and personnel support. Small, independent colleges experience this level of challenge far differently than large- state-funded and financially well-endowed private institutions of higher education. Nevertheless, these small engines of higher education that do a lions share of the educational work are especially good at doing a lot with a little. Full implementation of Competency Based Education is just one more challenge that will require creativity, efficiency and energy to meet. The following chart offers a diagram of what such an effort would entail.

A Model for Implementing Competency-Based Education

Competency-Based Education: A Conceptual Framework

Tool Skills Competencies	Service Areas Competencies	Professional Area Competencies
Written Oral Quantitative	General Knowledge	Professional Standards

Observable, Measurable Objectives	Teaching-Learning Strategies Discipline-Sensitive Student-Centered	Assessment Formative and Summative With Clearly Stated Criteria	Feedback and Intervention

Syllabus Conveys All of the Above

Three Centers of Initiative and Areas of Responsibility

Faculty: Curriculum standards and assessment development:	Administration and Board: Governance and Management:	Marketing & Institutional Research: Manage Marketing and Recruitment Issues
-develop an academically rigorous curriculum; -measure performance; -weighing curriculum options.	-create a organizational structure supportive of curriculum development; -manage personnel issues especially with regard to needed professional development; -develop internal policies that support implementation of CBE; -evaluate the implementation process; -manage growth; -address liability issues; -contract consulting services as needed to support professional development	-address (internally and externally) issues re: transcripts, placement and degree-audit; -represent the concerns institutional "markets" in implementation process; -coordinate media relations; -develop and maintain reporting mechanism; -report findings internally and externally; -develop literacy links with broader community; market the initiatives

Chapter 2

Implementing CBE into humanities' majors and General Education programs

Barbara Goodman

The Pleasure (and the bliss) of the Text

> Text of pleasure: the text that contents, fills, grants euphoria; the text that comes from culture and does not break with it [. . .] Text of bliss: the text that imposes a state of loss, the text that discomforts [. . .] unsettles the reader's historical, cultural, psychological assumptions, [. . .].[23]

When I was a child, there was no greater pleasure for me than lying on the glider on our screened in porch and reading books. When I went to college it seemed obvious to me that I would be an English major. What other major would have the homework assignment that consisted of "read a book"? I loved reading Eliot's *Middlemarch* and James's *The Ambassadors*. I liked to sit back and listen when it was clear the professor was discussing a beloved text. I took pleasure from seeing another's pleasure. Even now discovering a new book and reading is an indulgent, almost guilty pleasure; finding someone else who loves the book and discussing it with him or her can be one of my chief joys in life.

However, after 25 years of teaching English, I now know that not all students become English majors because of that personal joy. Yes, some students

---

[23] Roland Barthes, *The Pleasure of the Text,* trans. Richard Miller (New York: Hill and Wang, 1975) 14.

go into marketing, advertising, public relations and they've been told English is a good complement to their Communications major. Some English majors love books but different ones than I do—they love the post-modernist novelists and avant-garde texts and dislike my traditional English novelists and Renaissance playwrights; these are the students who resent the emphasis on the classics and argue for the need to update and revise the English major curriculum. They make challenging and exciting students as they want to discuss books but from a different perspective than I may be accustomed to.

All of these students are in my classes. All of them deserve the best I can give them in the classroom; yet all of their needs and expectations of the classroom differ. Silently (or not so silently) they send up the cries: "Teach me to think critically, to analyze and synthesize—I need it for law school"; "Teach me to understand Shakespeare and know the Romantic poets so I can pass the state certification test and teach high school," "Teach me the words to make my writing better so I can be famous, successful, great"; "Give me the knowledge I need so I can succeed in **my** dreams—because my dreams are not your dreams and my loves are not your love." Every student's desired outcome is as important as any other students—even if I personally identify with some more than others. And so after 25 years in the classroom, I can say with all honesty—it's not about my needs and my loves; it's about the students' needs and students' expectations.

Thus when in the midst of a contentious debate about General Education and its purpose—all of which was leading to revisions in the General Education program that would require to every department in the liberal arts and humanities to give up some of their treasured courses and closely defended turf—when a colleague announced that any person who hadn't read Shakespeare was not a well-educated person, I found myself questioning some of my longest held and most cherished beliefs. I teach the English major's Shakespeare course (and love it) but could I claim a computer professor who could do complex processes on the computer was less well educated than I am—when I have to call such a person almost every week with technology questions. What really is a well-educated person? If a student has read the Tang dynasty poetry of Li Po and the Vedas of ancient India but has not read Shakespeare is she less educated than an American high school student who has suffered through classes on *Romeo and Juliet* and *Macbeth*? What is a well-educated person today and what is the purpose of telling students they **must** take a literature or philosophy or even a math course? How can I make those General Education courses I so believe in and so love to teach relevant to the student who wants a degree in Accounting or Law Enforcement? How can I help the student become "well-educated" in the terms of the humanities courses I teach and yet make those courses relevant to their goals and expectations? And maybe even give them more than they expect with regard to their anticipated needs? For all of us in the humanities believe the true pleasure of the text is the unexpected discovery, the unanticipated insight that can change your perspective and alter your life.

The pleasure and the bliss of the text? It's still there—in the privacy of the book and the public domain of the classroom. The joy of the word? It's what inspires me in the classroom and makes my job so much fun. But meeting students' needs and expectations—that's what will make me a good teacher and successful professor. Finding a way to combine that pleasure, that love, and yet fulfill student expectations is what has led me to Competency Based Education. It is not mutually exclusive to the humanities' call to "the well-educated person" to the "exploration of creativity and insight into human nature." Instead it offers a way to bring together that intrinsic pleasure and student expectations. My enthusiasm and joy in the content of my course, my desire for students to find that same joy, my goal for students to gain insight into themselves and society and still allow for the unexpected or unanticipated discovery—these ambitions are not tempered by Competency Based Education, rather they are enhanced by what Competency Based Education offers the students and me as the deviser of the course curriculum.

42

A Philosophical Digression

For a brief time in college I considered being a philosophy major. I had a professor whose teaching style and enthusiasm for the subject inspired my interest. I, however, did not change my major from English when I realized it was the professor's approach and not the subject that I found interesting. However, one of the courses I took while considering this change was The Philosophy of Education. In this course I read such books as Freire's *The Pedagogy of the Oppressed* and Illich's *Deschooling Society*, along with seminal works by Plato, Dewey, and Piaget. For the first time I understood that there were theories to teaching and that these theories at times were radical, even revolutionary; contradictory, even antagonistic. Thus when I found myself many, many years later at an institution debating various approaches of education, I found my interest re-awakened and I listened carefully to those advocating for Competency Based Education, a philosophy I was not familiar with.

Digression 1: A "minor" Socratic Dialogue

Socrates . . . the ultimate example of a philosopher whose approach to life would seem to antithetical to the CBE method of teaching and education. And yet Socrates would have been the first to examine CBE beyond its stereotypes of "technical teaching" and "narrowness."[24] Socrates' method requires skepticism; it forces students to question, not to accept without doubt. The Socratic method involves a process of elimination—with better hypotheses being acknowledged, and contradictory or weak hypotheses being rejected. In order for the Socratic method to work, the teacher (questioner) and student must agree on the topic and the student must try to answer the teacher's questions using logical reasoning.[25] While CBE might not seem to be on the same high moral or intellectual plane as Socrates' dialogues on piety, courage or justice, it is an educational philosophy

---

[24] Bullough, Patterson, and Mayes.

[25] Wikipedia, the free encyclopedia, Google, 31 May 2005, 1 August 2005.

and as such is worthy of the same Socratic approach as any other philosophy which as its proponents and its detractors.

Q: Can we implement Competency Based Education in the humanities?

Student 1: Impossible—we offer more to the students than technical programs. Our field is more than just training students for the working world. We offer students a chance to know themselves.

Q: Who uses CBE successfully?

Student 1: Technical fields—training programs, medical schools, business schools, nursing schools

Q: But not the humanities?

Student 1: No.

Q: So how do you define CBE?

Student 1: CBE started in industry—where good training is imperative to successful corporate and industrial management: training for those skills necessary for improved productivity, better investment returns.

Q: Is that why there is resistance to CBE in the liberal arts and humanities? Because of its beginnings in industry's training programs?

Student 1: That's right. Industrial training and the humanities do not have the same goals—the same purpose—A liberal education is not preparation for a career. As Professor Leon Kass stated, its importance extends beyond acquiring "the skills of careful reading, writing, listening, speaking, arguing, calculating, looking, and experimenting."[26] He adds: "More simply liberal education is education in and for thoughtfulness. It awakens, encourages, and

---

[26] Leon Kass,"The Aims of Liberal Education" *The Aims of Education* (Chicago, U of Chicago P, 1997) 86.

renders habitual thoughtful reflection about weighty human concerns, in quest of what simply is true and good."[27]

Q: And this precludes implementing CBE?

Student 1: You can't measure that—

Student 2: You need to know if you are succeeding in whatever your goals are—that's what CBE allows you to do.

Student 1: But it doesn't allow you to reach those goals such as Professor Kass explains—

Q: How do you know you are succeeding in that wonderful goal?

Student 2: Wonderful goal? It's nothing but abstract irrelevance— and it means nothing without measurable assessment techniques.

Student 1: There's more to education than statistics and qualitative data.

Student 2: That's why it's all a shocking mess—

Student 1: It's all a glorious muddle—

Q: What is?

Student 1: The liberal arts in American colleges and universities

Student 2: And that's effective?

Student 1: What's effective mean? Professor Booth claims "The main goal of education [is] to liberate minds otherwise enslaved, by developing the skills first of recovering meanings, then rejecting the ones that do not hold up under a close look, and finally renovating, resynthesizing those that do."[28]

Q: Then you accept the terms Professor Booth uses such as developing, scrutinizing, re-synthesizing?

Student 1: Yes. Of course.

---

[27] Kass 86-87.

[28] Wayne C. Booth, "The Aims of Education" *The Aims of Education* (Chicago: U of Chicago P, 1997) 36.

Q: Those are concrete terms that are used in the language of competency-outcomes and assessment of those outcomes.

Student 2: So you need Competency Based Education in the liberal arts!

Q: But Booth's statement rejects narrowness and technical exclusivity in rejecting the enslaved mind.

Student 1 and 2: What are you saying?

Q: Simply, abstract thinking and philosophical thoughts are not minimized by concrete explanations and definitions. Indeed, concretizing philosophy is what makes ideas so powerful. In fact, Plato's "Allegory in the Cave" works because it is an allegory—a tangible representation of abstract ideas and concepts. It appears CBE and the humanities are no more mutually exclusive than abstract thought and concrete examples or allegory are for clarifying that abstract thinking.

Digression 2: Sic et Non

Peter Abelard, a monk living in 1100s, wrote a book entitled *Sic et Non* about the complexity of religious faith. This book offered "on one hand" and then "on the other hand" as it demonstrated the contradictory ideas and statements of various religious and Catholic scholars with regard to religious teachings. Abelard, the leading philosopher of logic who used *dialecta* in his argument, attempted to reconcile faith and reason. This attempt led him to be accused of heresy by other church members, most particularly Bernard of Clairvaux. Bernard argued that faith cannot be "reasoned"; he rejected out of hand the idea that faith could be "explained." This rejection out of hand, the belief that faith and reason are mutually exclusive, is similar to many of the professors in the humanities believing that the humanities and CBE are mutually exclusive. Bernard did not allow himself to examine Abelard's ideas fully. In his presentation of Abelard's heresies at the Council of Sens, he selected terms and

46

sentences from Abelard's books out of context—without considering or even understanding the full meaning of Abelard's arguments.

This same problem is found with the professors who reject Competency Based Education out of hand. They do not examine the philosophy and use of Competency Based Education fully. They rely on terminology or statements used out of context, and refuse or are afraid to consider the full implications of Competency Based Education. They examine its origins in industry and training and see it as narrow and constricting; they are not aware of its flexibility in usage. Perhaps one of the most perceptive remarks about CBE is made by in a report by Babson College, which "reinvented" its curriculum as a CBE curriculum: "[its curriculum] needed to become more rigorous, flexible, and able to instill in students a greater responsibility for their own intellectual and interpersonal growth"[29] As Abelard demonstrated in his book, *Sic et Non*, there can be a yes and a no, a one hand and other hand, when examining philosophical ideas, and as he sought to demonstrate through all his writings, the use of reason is not incompatible with faith or religion—nor is it incompatible with any of the other humanities in our higher education institutions. As Babson College learned, there can be flexibility and creativity, self-reflection and vigorousness examination with a competency based curriculum.

A return to the original digression. . .

Thus, as I listened to my colleagues' debates and arguments about CBE, I compared their ideas to what I had encountered in my classroom for over 25 years of teaching. I discovered that their arguments were not that far off from what I thought made good teaching already:

---

[29] Maria Ianozzi, "Babson College. Policy Perspectives. Exemplars," (Pew Higher Education Roundtable. Philadelphia: Institute for Research on Higher Education, 1998) 2, ERIC, EBSCO, Calumet College of St. Joseph, Specker Library, 1 August 2005. Babson is ranked as the top business college in the country (*U.S. News and World Report*) moreover, its recognition of the importance of the humanities in a business curriculum is laudable: "the first year Foundation program, which includes self-reflective work, integrated humanities and quantitative courses..." (1)

1.   constant revision—a course should never be static, but based on what works in the classroom and what doesn't, it should be modified and revised.

2.   attempted innovation—never be afraid to experiment or attempt new approaches or assignments in a course

3.   limited lecture—too much lecture is not good teaching

4.   legitimate explanations—students should know why this course is important and how it fits into their educational program

One aspect CBE underscored that I already was utilizing already in my classes was the importance of the feedback loop. The feedback loop is twofold: students demonstrating what they had learned (through essays, orals and tests) and letting me know (through surveys and conversation) what worked in the class and what didn't. Also I always welcomed and often instituted conversations on why students needed or were taking the course I taught. I truly believe that if you can't defend a course or an assignment's existence then you need to re-examine the rationale for offering that course or giving that assignment. CBE merely took this belief and made it more concrete: a program's competencies clarify the need for certain courses and a course's competencies clarify the need for certain assignments.

What CBE gave me that was new in my course was the need to clarify for students the assessment aspect of their assignments. Until that time, like many other teachers and professors, I would assign an A or a C on a paper, with comments and explanations, but I never gave the students a full explanation or criteria of what I wanted *beforehand*. In higher education too often professors (myself included) assume college students know what you want and what is expected. With CBE I realized I needed to define more clearly my expectations and to make sure these expectations were in line with my course and program competencies. My classes became fairer to my students as they now knew what I expected and could more readily work to achieve those expectations. CBE as a philosophy offered me more flexibility and more creativity—not less.

The actual usage of Competency Based Education in the humanities

How can you implement competency-based education and assessment into humanities and liberal arts? Or rather can you implement competency-based education without destroying the innate nature of humanities and liberal education? Implementing Competency Based Education into the humanities and liberal arts may actually comprise dealing with two elements of humanities education: the major and General Education curriculums. In my experience, the discussion of Competency Based Education began with a discussion of revamping our General Education program; however, the implementation of Competency Based Education and assessment has been far more successful in the majors than in the General Education program, even though General Education was altered quite thoroughly, it is not on a full competency based system nor were the revisions done through the backward design/forward implementation of the curriculum by letting the outcomes drive the curriculum.

As has been already discussed, the most noted uses of Competency Based Education have been in professional settings or in graduate programs for the professions. Many MBA, nursing, and medical schools have implemented CBE with great success. In particular, Australia, Canada and the United Kingdom have been leaders in this movement. Perhaps with their histories of external examinations and outside examiners, these institutions have been more willing to recognize the need for stated outcomes by which the students can measure their growth and their success. Otherwise without standardized criteria the use of external examiners would not only be arbitrary but also unfair. We in our institutions in the United States have always put much more emphasis on a professor's individualized evaluation and personal perception. These evaluations and perceptions are based on training and knowledge, of course, but still they are subjective by nature.

Exploring Successful Convergences of CBE and the Humanities

As Chapter One states, the term competency refers to the ability to be something. This ability can be to add a series of numbers, to dissect a frog, or to parse a sentence. This ability can be to diagnose a medical problem, discover shortfall in a company's financial statement, write a novel or create a painting. Guiding a student to discover that ability is a professor's role, and assessment of this ability is what the faculty member does, either through formative assessment or summative assessment, to analyze the level of that particular student's ability. In order for students to understand what a professor expected and for the professor's assessment to be effective, the outcomes have to be crystal clear.[30]

CBE: implementation into a humanity's major

In the introduction the waterfall/iterative model of Competency Based Education demonstrates the cyclical nature of implementing Competency Based Education into higher education. In the humanities, using the ideas of "backward design" leads the faculty to ask what do we want the students to be able to do/know at the end of the studies: the area to first explore is instructional design and the competencies that explain what we expect our students to be able to do when they finish our classes. We all have expectations of what the students will get out of our programs and their courses. The question is do these expectations match what the students require from our class for their future needs? And if they do, are we actually giving the students what they need? Are we fulfilling those expectations?

Developing a full program as a competency based program is an exciting and challenging experience. It does not happen immediately, nor should it. It takes time to discover what approach will work for implementing CBE into a program. For a humanities program, such as English, the early approach is invigorating and surprisingly straightforward. The main requirement is that all of the faculty (or at a larger institution, a great majority) be on board and ready to begin the experiment. First, there needs to be general agreement on the outcomes for the program. Our faculty started by developing overall competencies for the program by asking the question: what should an English major be able to do when

---

[30] See the discussion on competencies and their formulation in Chapter One.

he or she graduates? What knowledge? What abilities? But even more critical, what is it that defines him or her as an English major? How does the English major touch and change a person? These questions need to be explored at length by the faculty and then the beliefs need to be clearly stated. These statements of almost principles become the basis of the program's overall competencies. For our program we ended up with seven program competencies and then four-six further competencies for each specific concentration within the program.[31] These competencies then helped us design our course curriculums—

1. what courses were required for all majors,
2. which courses we required for only certain concentrations,
3. which courses should be electives.

It also caused us to eliminate some courses and add other courses. Thus, for our program, looking at the waterfall/iterative model found in the Introduction, we began with overall curriculum design and program competencies. These competencies are never set in stone. As the model demonstrates CBE necessitates constant, cyclical evaluation and modification. The competencies and the courses that have been developed are reviewed and redesigned constantly. Then the individual courses have the program competencies assigned to it through the mapping, and from those program competencies I personally also develop competencies specific to the individual courses.

With these program and course competencies, I then set out to design meaningful classroom activities and assessment criteria that will allow the students to achieve these competencies. Lecture alone does not work in a CBE humanities classroom. It may be an important manner for disseminating information but it is the least successful way of students retaining information.

---

[31] Our English program has three tracks or concentrations: literature/secondary education; creative writing; and journalism. See the end of the chapter for a copy of the competencies for the overall program and individual concentrations, as well as the course mapping for these competencies. Please be aware that these competencies and the mapping is constantly undergoing examination and revision and may have changed by the time this book is published.

Research has demonstrated that students retain only 5% of what they hear in lecture; so how can a professor—no matter how much he or she enjoys talking about the subject—believe he or she has fulfilled the students' expectations and needs for the class if they are walking away with only 5% of the disseminated material? But lecture accompanied with appropriate other activities, such as discussion, role playing, group discussion, allows a professor to make sure students not only absorbed the material but are also able to analyze and synthesize it. Certainly, student retention of information does not necessarily mean they understand it or are able to utilize it in a meaningful way. For example, a young student (in elementary school) sat in her history lesson and listened to her teacher explain how Texas broke away from Mexico and eventually became part of the United States. The young girl was able to do well on the test because she understood her teacher's words and was able to repeat them for the test. However, when explaining what happened to her aunt (me), she elaborated on her teacher's words and it became clear that her understanding was not as perfect as it seemed. She explained to her aunt that Texas had broken away and floated up to the United States. Texas had floated literally away from Mexico and joined with North America. When I tried to explain the broke away did not mean physically broke away and Texas did not float, she argued vehemently with me saying, "But Aunt Barbara, the teacher said it broke away and joined with the United States." As a young teacher myself (this was many years ago) I learned a valuable lesson—a student can understand your words, but completely misinterpret their meaning. This fact was brought home in my own classroom when I used the word "apse" in reference to architecture of a church. When defining the word, the definition offered by the dictionary was that an apse is a small recess in a church. A student proceeded to use the word in the following manner, "After the sermon we took a brief apse."—again the student understood the words of the definition but completely missed the meaning; recess to him meant a break from work or concentration such as recess time in elementary school. These two examples are not exclusive from what happens in a college classroom with straight lecture.

52

Students can take in the words but that does not mean they understand the meaning. Knowing the words students are able to pass objective tests but actually have no comprehension of what the class activity was supposed to teach—and no attainment of any true objectives and learning. This is a major reason why objective testing itself does not demonstrate even appropriate knowledge, let alone higher learning skills found on Bloom's Taxonomy, such as analysis and synthesis. Role-playing, group or individual discussions are all means to make sure that these inadvertent, but important, errors are not made by students and professors.

In CBE, there are two types of assessment: formative and summative. Humanities professors, seeing the statistical aspect sometimes found in summative assessment, forget the emphasis CBE puts on formative assessment. Formative assessment is a method of improving the quality of instruction and student learning.[32] It allows students to receive immediate feedback through class work, discussion, and peer evaluations. Certainly, one of the most important aspects in a humanities class, whether it is a literature, philosophy or theater arts class, is the element of discussion. As Socrates noted, through questioning and response, students learn to reason rather than depend solely on authority. An informal discussion can allow students to begin to demonstrate their abilities to reason and analyze, not just to reiterate back what a professor has stated. And certainly that dream goal—insight and growth of an individual—can only occur through students being encouraged to grow and not just mimic a professor's stance. While most classroom discussions may not reach the level of a Socratic dialogue, they are still strong teaching and learning tools. Informal discussion may or may not be assessed formally. Instead, a professor can use such moments to examine if the students are starting to express their own viewpoints—no formal analysis but a sense from the class attitude and awareness. More structured discussions allow students to express their perceptions of the issue and allow a

---

[32] See Chapter One.

teacher to guide their responses so that they may even gain greater insight. Yet such discussions are often difficult to assess. They are ephemeral, spontaneous, and sometimes a teacher can become so involved in talking that it unintentionally becomes a lecture/talk rather than a free flowing discussion.

A good discussion is one in which students are able to reflect their knowledge but also demonstrate their understanding, and possibly even expand their perspective. So how does a person formally assess a good discussion? You don't want to be constantly stopping the conversation to write down an evaluation, comment, or grade. You don't want to miss one student's response while writing down what another student has spoken. One method I have found which allows for free and open discussion and yet allows me to assess the discussion is to have student-led discussions. For example, in a Drama class I had each student choose a play they would lead a discussion on. The rest of the class had to read the play (and did) in order to have it discussed. The other students tended to read the plays for their classmates almost more than they did for their teacher—as they know their classmates' assessments depend on their participation—and their own evaluations depend on their classmates' participation. But in order to make sure the students knew how to lead an effective discussion, first I modeled such discussions. I handed out sample questions to the students, and I conducted the discussion in the same format that the student-led discussions would follow. I allowed the students to be a part of a sample discussion and then allowed them to ask me questions about the format and assessment so that they would feel comfortable with the process. This process did not work as well when I did not do a complete modeling session with questions prepared ahead of time in my Shakespeare class. I assumed that they understood the format and the technique—and once again assumptions proved wrong. While the Drama class discussions were stimulating and exciting for the students and easy for me to assess, the Shakespeare discussions tended to be labored and uninspiring. The students' preparations and consequent discussions were poor because I failed to model my expectations fully. Why did I fail to model properly? I ignored the basic requirements of CBE—to make the outcomes clear in measurable, observable terms and presented at the outset. I gave the students a rubric/criteria but I did not make those outcomes clear in observable fashion nor did I present them at the outset. A list of expectations, without thorough explanation or modeling, was not enough. I fell back into the old trap of "assuming" the students would know what I wanted—a dangerous assumption as it hurt the students' abilities to achieve the course and program competencies as laid out in the curricular design.

This assignment is an excellent example of competency based summative assessment that allows for a full, unhindered discussion as is preferred in a humanities class and builds on the formative assessment/discussion earlier in the course. By removing the teacher from role of teacher, it allows the teacher to focus on the discussion, concentrate on appropriate assessment and not to talk too much and hinder student comments. Yet a teacher can answer a student question or comment or add a comment or two as a part of the discussion. Through modeling and giving the students examples of questions and a rubric for evaluation you are participating in CBE assessment. Yet the activity is what faculty enjoy being a part of in the humanities—the process of exploration and discovery. Moreover, this approach allows students to emphasize what they need from the text and the class—allowing them to approach the text in a manner that is relevant to their outcome expectations.

All discussion need not be assessed—there is nothing that indicates pure class discussion without formal assessment is not beneficial or that it doesn't help reach course competencies. Sometimes, especially early in the semester, students need to be able to explore without concern of assessment. These discussions often surprisingly lead students to developing a stated outcome. For example, in a seminar I was teaching on Folklore and Fairy Tales, the students chose many of the folktales we were to read. Most of the students were upper level students who had requested this elective seminar and thus were motivated to become leaders in the course development. While I chose the various approaches we would take in the course (historical, oral tradition, modern interpretations such as Freudian or Feminist), the student selected the works themselves. In our fourth week of the course, unintentionally, we found our discussion on "Jack and the Beanstalk" came around the same day we were discussing Freudian interpretation. The discussion was to be an informal discussion with no formal assessment tool employed. The plan was for us to discuss the folktale and then apply the Freudian theory of folktales we had read to this tale. It was an opportunity for me to begin to see if the students were able to link literary theory, oral traditions and folktales. Later in the semester, there was planned summative assessment applications of this task through written essays and oral presentations, but this early in the semester any assessment would be extremely informal and formative to gauge the students' understanding and ability to synthesize these aspects of literature. The discussion between eight women (seven students and me) became rowdy and even raunchy as it covered issues from penis envy to masturbation. I mention this class because students later were able to take this casual (yet very lively) discussion and build on it in order to demonstrate their achievement of their course outcomes. Student PowerPoint presentations later in the semester would reflect this success of the earlier informal discussion. Their presentations were well developed and lively, demonstrating a keen ability to analyze and synthesize diverse literary texts and literary theories. Students, semesters later, would refer back to that class discussion as one of the most outrageous and yet fascinating discussions they had had in a literature class. Thus, a totally unplanned class discussion became the springboard to a successful CBE planned course and assessment.

A humanities class that is taught with CBE is not that different than a typical humanities class in many ways: the same material can be covered, the same books may be used, even assignments (essays, oral presentations) can be the same—yet the heart of the class can be changed as all of those elements are organized in a different manner.

56

First—the focus must be student-centered. The focus must be on what outcomes the students achieve at the end of the course—or if it's part of a CBE program, what outcomes of the program this course is expected to help the students achieve.

Second—all assignment/assessment should in some way measure whether or not the students reached these outcomes.

Third—students should be familiar with both the outcomes and the criteria for assessment so that they and the professor are working together to achieve those outcomes.

Fourth—new or unexpected outcomes may emerge as the professor and the students work together—outcomes that enrich both of their experiences in that course.

Fifth—flexibility in the classroom allows for outcomes to be achieved, sometimes through means not anticipated at the beginning of the course. After all, every class develops a persona—as students interact with each other, the professor and the content matter—and you as the professor do not know what that persona will be at the beginning of the class. Every professor knows a course can have the same exact coursework and assignments as another, yet due to the dynamics among the students and between the professor and the students, the two courses may be as different as night and day. The use of competencies makes sure the class stays on tracks yet allows a class to emerge as its own dynamic entity—

A SUMMARY: Designing a Competency Based Education program in a majors program in the humanities

> 1. Backward design/forward implementation: e.g. what should a graduating English major know or be able to do at graduation: These are your program competencies
> 2. What courses and other activities (e.g. colloquia) do you need to offer to achieve these program competencies? These

courses and activities form your program curriculum both prerequisites, requisites and electives

3.   Mapping: Which courses support which competencies? You need to make sure that all the competencies are addressed within the program curriculum you have developed, and the professors involved need to know which courses are expected to cover which competencies. Mapping makes sure all the program competencies are covered. If not, other courses and activities may need to be developed (we actually expanded our program by five courses and added three requisites after doing these first three steps).

4.   Course competencies are derived from the program competencies that were mapped for individual courses. Course competencies may be more specific and more elaborate than the actual program competencies.

5.   Coursework and Assignments: these are what students do in order to achieve the competencies. For example, in a literature course the coursework may be the reading list and assignments that vary from discussion to oral presentations to essays and research papers to quizzes and exams.

6.   Assessment: this is what you do (as professor) to assure that students have achieved the competencies. The assessment methods consist of criteria-standards that students are expected to achieve and rubrics for evaluating these standards.

This simple approach allows for a full and comprehensive development of a competency based program, whether it is in the professional fields or the humanities. For the humanities, the important aspect is to start with the overall view—backward curriculum design, e.g. starting at where the students end, allows the faculty to develop a full and exciting discussion of what an English major (or any other humanities program) is for—addressing the often asked question—why major in ... (fill in the humanities) or even more frustrating question—what can you do with a major in... (fill in the humanities program) as if the only reason you major in a program in college is because of your need "to do" something. The answer to the question, why major in . . . need not be "to get a job in..." but can easily be "because you love it," "because it excited you,"—but that "lack of career plan" does not mean that a student at the end of the major shouldn't expect certain abilities and skills to be developed; indeed, critical thinking and creative thinking are abilities and skills as much as programming a computer or balancing a ledger. In fact, in the humanities it is even more important to have outcomes because those outcomes are so much more difficult to define and achieve.

The most exciting part of CBE after developing and implementing the program is its feedback loop, which is built into the system. Because of the way the program curriculum is designed, faculty inevitably will find themselves needing to and wanting to revise and restructure the program to make it more effective. The feedback loop works on many levels:

1. do the assessment and assignments accurately measure competency (redesign assignments and/or assessment)

2. does the coursework accurately cover its expected program competencies (redesign coursework or competencies)

3. are the competencies appropriate for the course (redesign competency mapping)

4. is the course appropriate for the competencies (redesign curriculum)

5. are the program competencies appropriate for the expected outcomes of a graduating English major (redesign program competencies)

6. are our English majors achieving those program competencies/outcomes (redesign program competencies or curriculum)

The feedback loop is constant and continual—modifications are always being made according to the answers to the questions—modifications in assessment methods, modifications of assignments and course work, modification in program curriculum and modifications in program competencies/outcomes.

CBE: implementation in General Education/Core courses

John Proctor in his book *Defining the Humanities* states that one dilemma facing higher education is the inability to define exactly what should be taught—especially in the humanities. "No one today knows what the humanities are. [. . .] The phrase 'the humanities' warms almost everyone's heart. But why can't we define them?"[33] Proctor also sees a problem with the emphasis today on methodology instead on content: "Today, the accolades and the prestigious careers often go to those who seem most adept in inventing new techniques of analysis and research."[34] Proctor's concerns summarize many humanities professors, including my own, when I first started using CBE in my classroom. With so much debate on content, why was I focusing on methodology? What I found, however, was the CBE embraced content and methodology—that the two were not disparate but rather intertwined. The discussion about CBE in the humanities inevitably led to the discussion about content and what should be a part of a complete "Core" or "general Education" curriculum. CBE forces one to examine one's underlying assumptions about what is or is not needed in the curriculum as one is attempting to decide how to implement that material.

Almost all undergraduate institutions have a series of courses that are known as either "the core curriculum" or "General Education." These courses are required courses for all undergraduates no matter what their major or course of studies. These programs, whether required interdisciplinary courses or a more menu approach, are designed with the idea that students need these basic knowledges and skills in order to be "better" or "more complete" students. Yet

---

[33] John Proctor, *Defining the Humanities: How Rediscovering a Tradition can Improve Today's Students* (Bloomington: Indiana UP, 1998) xxiii

[34] Proctor xxv.

often students resent these courses. An pre-med student may ask why he needs to read *Gilgamesh*; an accountant student may ask why she needs to study Greek philosophy. For humanities professor, often one or two of the courses we teach every semester, in small liberal arts colleges, consist of these General Education/Core classes. The same issues that are raised in a majors class—why do I need this class—how will it help me—are raised in General Education/Core classes yet with more hostility or resentment. In English majors classes, a student may not want to read Chaucer or study the History of the English Language, but at least he or she is in some way interested in the major or the subject itself. But in the General Education/Core classes, there are students who are not interested in the subject at all, who resent even being in the class. CBE can help give students an understanding of the purpose and the rationale for these required courses, and can help instructors develop a full and relevant curriculum.

Developing a CBE program for General Education courses is more complex and difficult than developing one for a specific major program. These courses involve faculty from a wide variety of disciplines, philosophies, and programs. Each faculty member brings his or her own perspective and own biases to the discussion. Developing competencies for such a program is not easy. In order to do so it takes open minds and lively debate. Starting at the same point as when developing a CBE program in a major, the question has to be asked: what do we expect of a student after he/she has gone through the General Education/Core program? What defines a student who has completed a General Education program? The curriculum should again be designed backward— starting at the outcome and working backward to develop the competencies and courses, and only then implemented forward. These competencies can determine content, certainly help drive the discussion of content—defining, as Proctor desires, what the humanities are and how they operate in college's curriculum. This means that you begin with NO assumptions about what courses need to be offered; all courses are possible; all courses are on the table until the desired outcomes and desired competencies are developed. It is not easy to do with such a diverse group of faculty members with such diverse interests and viewpoints. I believe developing a CBE General Education/Core program could be one of the most exciting prospects in higher education, but it could also be one of the most painful and antagonistic. It certainly cannot be imposed; it can only emerge from a flexible faculty that has embraced the potential and possibility of CBE and sees it as a way of re-creating a better program and not just strengthening an existing program. Babson College's experience, as discussed earlier, demonstrates it can be done. It is, however, not an activity for the faint-hearted or the firmly entrenched.

The first element necessary is for those involved in currently teaching the General Education/Core courses to recognize a need to improve or modify the program. If the overwhelming majority does not see such a need then you are setting yourself up for a contentious and ultimately unsuccessful endeavor. Often decrees to revise General Education come from administration, which can lead to greater resistance than if the decision comes from the General Education faculty itself.

Of course the General Education faculty is itself diverse, coming from a wide body of disciplines. Most of the faculty do not see themselves as General Education professors but rather as professors of their discipline, be it English, History, Math or Philosophy. Some may resist the common denominator of being lumped together as "General Education." A good practice is to have meetings of the General Education faculty throughout the year so that when the issue of revision comes up, there is already a consensus or identity established. If the faculty number is large, then one-two members from each discipline could function as representatives of the whole.

Once there is recognition that revision is necessary and the faculty identify with the task at hand, then the process of developing a fully coherent curriculum with trans-discipline competencies and appropriate courses established through mapping can begin. As stated before everything is on the table—no course is sacrosanct!

In designing a "backward design/forward implementation" curriculum for General Education, the same process can be followed that is followed by designing a curriculum for the major. Begin with the age-old questions: What is the purpose of General Education? What should a student who has completed the General Education courses know/be able to do/perform? The answers to these questions are what establish the General Education competencies. These competencies are *not* the competencies of individual courses or disciplines. They are the competencies that define what the outcomes of a General Education program are. Often a General Education includes two types of courses: skill courses (writing, speech, computer) and discipline/knowledge courses (literature, history, philosophy). The competencies established need not be divided into these two areas. A faculty may see General Education as a more integrative program and so choose to establish integrative competencies. However, if the faculty prefers a more separate approach that can be accommodated: skill competencies and knowledge competencies can be divided up. However, the problem becomes with competencies that involve elements of critical thinking—a skill that requires content and knowledge. Whatever manner the faculty chooses to approach the program competencies, no discussion of individual courses or disciplines should intrude on this discussion. Ideas and suggestions should be sought from other faculty, as they too have views on why students complete a General Education program. This is the most important part of the planning—do not rush through it. Allow differences to surface and discuss them fully.[35] If the principles and justification for a General Education program cannot be established—then it just becomes a matter of "take these courses because. . ."! And no education is a good education if there is no valid reason for its existence. Moreover, the establishment of sound, solid competencies for the overall General Education program will make it easier to develop the actual courses.

---

[35] Moreover surfacing differences at this time and not when establishing the actual courses can take much of the contentiousness and "turf protecting" out of the discussion. If everyone (or almost everyone) agrees on the program competencies, then establishing the courses that will allow those competencies to be met becomes more agreeable

The actual course requirements/curriculum becomes the goal with the mapping of the competencies and courses. The mapping of General Education courses with the competencies leads to the issue of whether the courses should interdisciplinary/integrated or discipline-specific. Should critical thinking be a separate course or integrated with other courses' content. If it is integrated, how do you assess students are achieving the competency of critical thinking. In a lower level General Education course (100/200 levels) can you expect students to achieve higher levels of critical thinking (e.g. synthesis)? If you teach critical thinking as a separate course, how do you make sure its skill is reinforced in the other courses, so that students' utilize the skill they are learning? These are just a few examples of the issues that are raised when developing a competency based General Education course. The diversity of faculty and the disciplines represented at the table, as well the differing philosophies on General Education's purpose and effect, lead to complex matters and difficult questions—but these matters and questions are not irresolvable. Just be aware of the problems that may arise, so that you can be prepared to work them out.

Overall, before developing the syllabi and competencies of the individual courses, the following areas need to be discussed and resolved:

1.   What is the purpose of General Education

2.   What should a student be able to do or know after completing a General Education program

3.   How does General Education enlighten and inform students

4.   After answering these questions, you should be able to develop a handful of all-encompassing competencies for the program as a whole

5.   After developing the competencies, other issues need to be resolved before the mapping begins:

   a. Are the skills and content courses to be separated into different areas with regard to curriculum and competencies

64

      b. Are the courses to be interdisciplinary/integrated courses or discipline-specific

      c. Are there any other (non-programmatic) concerns, such as

        i.Credit limitations (number of courses that can be offered)

        ii.Scheduling conflicts with other college courses

        iii.Should students be required to take General Education courses in their first two years or should some of the courses be upper-level courses involving higher critical thinking skills and thus taken later in their academic career

Only after discussing (perhaps arguing) at length about these issues and reaching some resolution are you ready to:

- develop the courses and utilize the program competencies to develop individual competencies for the courses

- develop assessment techniques that are appropriate for the individual courses .and competencies

Perhaps one of the biggest subjects in General Education is the question of assessment. Too often in General Education programs the attempt is made to dictate one type of assessment tool: portfolios, external written exams, standardized tests—they all have their proponents. Perhaps one of the ways in which Competency Based Education is most flexible is its recognition of the importance of the diversity of assessment tools, both formative and summative. An appropriate use of portfolio assessment in one course may not work at all in another course. A professor needs to develop the assessment tools that work to assess the competencies that are found within her course. Of course professors who teach the same course with the same competencies may choose to develop overall assessment tools that will be used in those classes. For example, in our first semester freshman composition course we applied the developed General Education competencies to a rubric and an end-of-semester writing competency essay that students need to pass in order to pass the course. Every year, the professors and writing instructors who teach freshman composition meet and hammer out any revisions found necessary. It is, to be honest, usually a very contentious and dynamic meeting. In the end we revise the competencies if necessary, modify the rubric as desired, and develop the essay test that all the students will take. In that class, we have even standardized the syllabi to a certain extent in order to clarify what aspects of essay writing should be emphasized and underscored in preparation for the final essay. However, in our integrated courses General Education courses, entitled Global Perspectives, we do not have the same regimentation. We have the established General Education competencies, but each professor determines her own curriculum (what works will be read, which books will be used) and what assessment tools will be used to assess the students' achievement of the competencies. In these courses, only the competencies that the students are expected to attain in the courses are consistent. Naturally, we share our ideas and our class assignments and assessment tools. We meet every year to discuss the courses and to share ideas. From these meetings, we have developed a course Web Page that we all use and also various shared assignments and readings.

As can be seen, even the approach to the individual courses (whether required, prescribed curriculum and assessment tools or flexible, less regimented curriculum and assessment tools should be used) can lead to yet more intense discussion and possible conflict. We as professors tend to be very individualistic and do not like prescriptive curriculum, yet if a group together develops that shared curriculum and assessment tool/s, then they are not being imposed but rather are a result of reached consensus. Use of shared curriculum and tools or individualized curriculum and tools need not be across the board—what works for some courses may not work for others, especially if you are working with interdisciplinary, integrated courses.

There is no doubt that any revision of General Education is a difficult process, fraught with many pitfalls and possible stumbling blocks. If the decision is made to revise the General Education program to be competency based, be prepared for it to be a long process—if it is to be done well. Also be prepared for

66

it to be a constant process; as the introduction with its waterfall/iterative model illustrates, a true competency based program is under constant modification as competencies, assignments and assessment tools are revised to better serve the students and the program's overall competencies.

In Conclusion

To complete the circuit of discussion—can CBE be implemented in humanities and General Education programs? Of course. Does it limit or hinder the creative or critical thinking so valued by humanities professors? Of course not. Instead, it is incumbent on humanities professors to delve beyond the "training" history of CBE and see how it can free up the discussion of content, purpose and curriculum that so often dominate the debate on the worth of the humanities as majors and as a part of General Education. To finish with the words of Roland Barthes:

> The pleasure of the text: like Bacon's simulator, it can say *never apologize, never explain.* It never denies anything: "I shall look away, that will henceforth be my sole negation."[36]

Anything that can make a humanities program, whether it be a majors program or General Education/core program more effective and more enticing to students is worth investigating and worth utilizing. To reject out of hand a pedagogy just because of its "training roots" is unworthy of those of us who claim to desire for students to delve—to explore—to discover—and ultimately to be transformed by these experiences. CBE offers us the means by which we can achieve these abstract yet critically important goals in our chosen field.

---

[36] Barthes 3.

Examples of competency based course assignments and assessment tools

Sample Assignment 1: The Drama Class assignment and sample questions

The Drama: Class Discussion

<u>Assignment</u>: Each student is responsible for leading the class discussion on his/her chosen play. The student will demonstrate his/her

- o knowledge of drama and this playwright/play's importance in drama history

- o ability to analyze a play's characters, themes, and dramatic issues

- o ability to synthesize through connecting the play to its historical context and its significance in relationship to other plays we have read.

<u>Assessment</u>: The student will be evaluated on the following:

1. Brief introduction of playwright and summary of play (5 points)
2. Series of discussion points or questions (10 points)
   a. Quantity (# appropriate for discussion)
   b. Relevance (as relates to text)
   c. Understanding (as relates to text)
   d. Connection (with other texts/plays we've read)
3. Commentary/replies to other student/classmate's points or questions (5 points)

<u>Notes</u>: The presentation/discussion should last 20-30 minutes for each play. Students will not be evaluated on their classmates' performance (e.g. classmates' responses or readings of the plays).

Finally, the assignment will be modeled in class with a discussion of

1. *The Misanthrope*
2. *The Rover*

Sample questions will be distributed as part of the modeling/discussion.

Sample Questions to Model Student-led Classroom Discussion of

Plays

The Misanthrope (Moliere)

1. Can an absolute interpretation of human behavior ever work?
2. Is Alceste's view or Philinte's view more desirable?
3. Is love ever "rational"?
4. Is Alceste's desire for control a demonstration of moral righteousness or moral narrow-mindedness
5. Compare/Contrast Alceste to Malvolio (Twelfth Night)—what happens to people who determine only their moral values are the right ones?
6. Compare and Contrast Alceste to Agememnon: why can neither see there might have been another way?
7. Discuss of issues/themes:
    a. rational vs. irrational
    b. absolutism vs. relativism
    c. social behavior vs. individual behavior (etiquette vs. "plainspeaking")
    d. male vs. female
    e. money vs. love

The Rover (Aphra Behn)

1. What themes are similar between these two plays? Different (e.g. reputation vs. sex)
2. How do the women compare in the two plays?
3. Is there any "moral" man in The Rover? Or is every man only interested in lust?
4. How does the play remind you of Twelfth Night? (money, arranged marriages, etc.) or other Shakespeare Plays? How is it different?
5. Do you think the play read "differently" because it was written by a woman? Would you have known if you hadn't been told?
6. Who is "The Rover"?
7. What are the political implications of the play?
8. Does the comedy remind you at all of medieval comedy (2nd shepherd or Noah)?
9. Do you think having "actual" women on stage changed the type of plays/humor being performed on stage?

Sample 2: General Education—Global Perspectives Portfolio Assignment, Grading Sheet and example of rubric

Portfolio: Global Perspectives

<u>Assignment</u>: Each student will develop a portfolio on a chosen country in Africa, Asia or the Middle East. The portfolio will consist of "artifacts"—each of which will be assessed according to the given criteria (rubric). This portfolio will be submitted in <u>hard copy</u>, but <u>also with a disk</u> that contains your own written work.

<u>Choose a country/region:</u>

Korea

Vietnam

Thailand

Japan

Tibet

Pakistan

Afghanistan

Turkey

Israel/Palestine

Iran

Iraq

Saudi Arabia

Ethiopia

Sudan

Kenya

Nigeria

Zimbabwe

South Africa

Liberia

<u>Note</u>: If another country in these regions interests you, you may choose that country with approval of the instructor. Some countries are not available as we are studying them in-depth in class.

<u>Artifacts and due dates</u>:

The following items will be included in the portfolio and will be due on the assigned week.

1. <u>Chronology</u> (3000BC to present)   Due week 4

> There must a minimum of 25 items;
> the items can be political, social, economic,
> religious, literary, or of the arts.
> Diversity is good!

2. <u>Modern situation/current position</u>   Due week 8

> Find two articles on your country's
> current situation (post 1940s). The
> articles should be 4-8 pages long—one should be
> a general article (maybe from the encyclopedia about
> country's government and general current situation)
> and the other on a <u>specific</u> current topic.
> <u>SUMMARIZE the two articles in ONE SUMMARY</u>
> in your own words; then state what the U.S. position is
> on this issue. The length must be 4+ pages.

3. <u>Literary Report</u>   Due week 13

> Read a novel/fiction work by an author
> from your country (post-1890s) and
> and write an essay (5+ pages) according
> to what the rubric requires.

4. <u>Complete bibliography/works used</u> (MLA format)   Due with <u>each</u> artifact submission

<u>Extra credit</u>: Select 5 current event articles about your country with 5-10 sentence summary of/reaction to article's content. (1 point per article up to 5 articles)

<u>Final completed (revised) portfolio</u>: Due week 15 (final test/exam day!).

Each submitted artifact will receive an evaluation/grade at its first submission. The artifact can

be revised for re-evaluation with the final portfolio submission.

Portfolio Grading Sheet

	Portfolio Format & Source Material	Chrono-logy	Current Situation Summary Essay	Literary Text and Essay	(Extra Credit)
Submitted on time (late deduct one-two pt. per week)					
Possible Score	Loss of up to 5 pts. if material is missing	5	5	10	5
Assigned Score					

Portfolio Rubric Part 1—Artifact 4

The Literary Essay

<u>Essay question</u>:

Discuss how your chosen piece of literature either reflects or challenges the cultural, historical, and social times (or events) in which it was composed.

In your introduction you must include:

1. name of literary work and author
2. very brief info on author (if known)
3. very brief info on country/region you are discussing
4. background about work, including protagonist, antagonist, setting (place and time)
5. thesis (whether work reflects or challenges)

In your main body you must include:

1. conflicts, themes and issues which refer to the essay question (e.g. individual vs. society)
2. economic, historical, and cultural information which relate book to country
3. any other information relevant to the question with regard to your work

In your conclusion you must include:

1. reference to at least one other work we read and how your work compares
2. reiterate your thesis and how you have proved your points

Paper requirements:

1. minimum of 5 (full) typed pages (1 inch margins, double-spaced)
2. quotations from the literary text to prove your points
3. good mechanics and sentence structure
4. all characters names, titles, authors, countries MUST be spelled correctly and dates must be accurate or the paper will be considered a #4 (see attached criteria).

Portfolio Rubric: Part 2— Artifact 4

The Literary Essay

This scale indicates roughly where your paper falls. More precise information can be found from the comments on your paper and from part 1 of the rubric.

F Papers: #1-4, possible points 0-5

1. The paper is dishonest/plagiarized (automatic 0).

2. The paper completely ignores the set/given essay question.

3. The paper is incomprehensible due to serious errors in language and grammar/mechanics.

4. The paper contains very serious factual errors.

D Papers: #5-6, possible points 6

5. The paper simply narrates storyline or repeats what was discussed in class and includes factual errors.

6. The paper contains no introduction, conclusion and has no concrete proof of points.

D/C Papers: #7-8, possible points 6-7

7. The paper simply narrates storyline or repeats what was discussed in class, and makes little or no attempt to frame an argument or thesis.

8. The paper states a thesis but it is one which does not address the /given essay question.

C Papers: #9-10, possible points 7

9. The paper states an argument or thesis but supporting points and evidence/proof are:
   a. missing
   b. incorrect
   c. irrelevant
   d. not specific enough
   e. partly obscured by errors in grammar and mechanics

10. The paper lacks either an introduction or a conclusion.

B Papers: #11, possible points 8

   11. The paper states a thesis on an appropriate topic, contains an introduction and a

conclusion, states supporting and relevant points, but

    a. factual evidence is either missing or not specific enough

    b. quotations/proof are given but are not explained

    c. points/ideas are not developed completely

    d. some factual evidence is incorrect

A Papers: #12, possible points 9-10

12. The paper states a thesis on an appropriate topic, contains an introduction and a conclusion, states supporting and relevant points and

    a. the ideas and points are original and well thought-out

    b. the proof is relevant, correct, and supports points

    c. the quotations/proof are clearly and coherently related to stated points

English Major and Individual Concentration Competencies

Upon completion of the English and Professional Writing major at Calumet College of St. Joseph, a student will be able to:

General Competencies:

1. Analyze and interpret works of literature of major writers that reflect diverse genres, time periods, and cultures

2. Examine the nature of the English language and how that nature influences developments in literature and writing

3. Demonstrate the ability to do research and writing that pertains to the multifaceted discipline of English and Professional Writing (e.g. literary, historical, legal)

4. Write coherently and creatively, making conscious and sophisticated stylistic choices in language and structure

5. Engage intellectually and creatively within the discipline of English and/or Professional Writing

6. Evaluate literary works within the context of the evolution of the ideas on social justice

7. Analyze and reflect upon human experience through reading and understanding great literary works and the writings of major authors

Literature/Secondary Education Competencies:

1. Communicate an understanding of literary criticism and use its frameworks to analyze and evaluate works of literature
2. Identify the development and application of various literary genres
3. Identify how literature reflects and challenges the values of the cultural and historical framework in which it was composed
4. Demonstrate how the forms and ideas of literature from previous ages are applicable to today's social context

Creative Writing Competencies:

1. Develop a strong clear voice and sense of audience in writing
2. Develop content, point of view and multiple techniques in writing
3. Write in diverse genres and forms (e.g. poetry, prose)
4. Prepare/develop piece of writing in the appropriate form and style for publication

Journalism Competencies:

1. Develop and apply a variety of interview techniques
2. Write in a manner appropriate for publication in newspapers/journals
3. Edit in a manner appropriate for publication in newspapers/journals
4. Utilize electronic technology as appropriate in the journalism profession
5. Understand and apply the legal and ethical responsibilities of journalism as a profession

Chapter 3

Darren Henderson

CBE an Inward Journey

Like most people that went through a "professional studies" curriculum, I did not have any formal training to be a teacher. My engineering education gave me technical training in mathematics, science, and computers to name a few areas but my idea of a teacher was drawn primarily from my own experiences as a student and through observing my own teachers. My own values and beliefs also invariably helped to shape the notion of what it means to be a teacher and what I deemed as the responsibilities of a student.

Teaching initially meant emulating my college professors. When I first began teaching I saw my role as predominately to be the "content expert" in whatever subject I was teaching (as my professors had been). Teaching meant thoroughly studying the material so that one could field the "tough questions" that might get hurled at you. Then teaching meant presenting the material in a similar way in which it had been presented to me. I assumed that most likely the students would not comprehend the material on the first exposure, since this tends to be the situation with difficult technical subjects. I further assumed that my students would endeavor to study the material on their own until they finally grasped it. Of course, I could facilitate this process by making my initial explanations as clear and cogent as possible. In addition, I could show them any potential pitfalls so that they could hopefully avoid them.

Unfortunately, I was soon confronted with the reality that my students did not study the material as much as I would have wanted them to. They were either unwilling or unable to spend an amount of time comparable to which I had regularly expended as a student. For me, I viewed going to college as my "job" in a sense. I was fortunate enough not to have to juggle other obligations like a family or employment. I was therefore able to concentrate my energies primarily on learning.

So this juxtaposition of the "reality" of my students' predicament and the "world view" of a teacher that I seemed to possess lead eventually to the realization that something had to give. What that turned out to be was my initial simplistic notions about what it meant to be a teacher. The transformation was initiated or motivated in part by a value and pride in the quality of my work, which made me receptive to changing my teaching methods if it appeared that they were unsuccessful. However, a useful "vehicle" for continued systematic change has been following the "path" of Competency Based Education (CBE). Doing so has resulted in and continues to have a profound impact on my teaching and has gradually transformed my thinking of what it means to be a teacher.

My experience with CBE can be characterized by transitions through a series of discrete stages. Although this pattern was not apparent throughout most of my experience, this visualization only occurred to me later after much reflection. The first stage I categorize as the initial exposure to the ideas and concepts of CBE. Next, there was some early experimentation in implementing CBE. This experimentation occurred over many cycles or iterations, which gradually lead to the next key stage, an internalization of the basic concepts of CBE. This stage was signified by the development and hence internalization of the "waterfall model" of CBE. The final stage is the continued application of CBE. I understand this final stage also to be iterative.

I was first exposed to the concepts underlying CBE during a faculty workshop at the college. At the time, I instinctively attempted to associate CBE concepts with things in the domain of my own experience, with things that I was familiar with or could relate to. For someone with no formal training in education, this act turned out to be critical in beginning the process of assimilation. Many of my initial impressions about CBE were that the concepts did not strike me as revolutionary. My engineering education undoubtedly had given me an affinity for such concepts. These concepts seemed to be largely common sense and what good teachers do anyway.

My initial exposure to CBE was significant in two respects. For one, as described above, it allowed me to begin to make connections with things that I was familiar with. Secondly, it began to immerse me in the language of CBE. For example, when learning about competencies, it struck me as a sound practice to write competencies that were clear and precise. I had always believed and tried to have a practice that "objectives" on a syllabus should be accurate (i.e. actually state what is done in the course) and complete. So, I saw the inherent value in the communicative aspects of competencies. The next point that stood out was the differentiation between formative and summative assessments. Initially, I mistakenly associated "formative assessments" with homework assignments that an instructor gives and "summative assessments" with the exams. In my experience, both homework assignments and exams would receive a grade. I now understand formative assessments to be more accurately described as ungraded learning opportunities for students. Another significant point in the workshop was the desirability of rubrics. From the presentation, I understood rubrics as vehicles to be able to evaluate/score students and to do so in an objective manner. Again, this was something that I felt I was already adept at since when grading an assignment, I tended to break down an assignment into point values and I was very mathematical about it. Again at the time, I did not think too much of the whole CBE thing since it seemed to be what I really was already doing for the most part.

However, I think the real breakthrough came when I was able to understand/grasp the totality of the CBE model. Competencies are what we want students to be able to do. Assessments either give students learning opportunities to practice or master a competency before they are evaluated for a grade (formative assessment) or are how teachers verify that the student achieves the outcome or competency (summative assessment) Rubrics are the set of standards or criteria used to evaluate the student's work. When I was able to embrace/internalize this model then it gradually began to change how I looked at things. For every event that occurred in a class, I began to analyze, what was the problem? Was it that I was not clear about what I was trying to get students to learn? Was it that I did not give them enough opportunities to practice a given skill before testing them? Was it that the test was not actually probing the areas of the student's knowledge and skills that I wanted to get at? What happened was that by embracing a model/process for teaching, I had something that I could follow, so I got caught up in it. The practice of implementing CBE was at first almost forced but gradually over time became more routine and then almost unconscious. I found that it was a rich model in that I could start at any point in the process and still yield useful results and that the results would feedback into changing my teaching and thereby hopefully impact the student's learning. The iterative nature of the model meant that as a teacher you can make small incremental changes over time: in a class, in an assessment, in a course, and that given enough time the end result is that the product is continually refined and improved. Tirelessly focusing on the CBE process can even lead to more than changes in the work product, it can even result in the teacher and hopefully the students being transformed.

My experience with CBE as an inward journey was due to where I started. I had to first become a teacher with CBE's help. I had to concentrate on what I was going to do in a class, in a course first. Only when I had a strong handle on this could I begin to move outward and be more receptive to how student's where doing/learning. I believe I am better in this regard than when I started but it is a never-ending journey. It is only through this inward journey that I feel that I am on the path of continual improvement as a teacher. Embracing CBE means embracing continual refinement, continual examination, all with the goal to be a better teacher so that students will learn better.

Having internalized the basic elements found in the waterfall model of CBE produces the situation where I continually challenge the efficacy of my teaching. As an example, just recently, I was reviewing the instructor materials for a chapter on CPU and Memory for the Hardware/Software Concepts course that I teach. As I was reviewing the PowerPoint handouts from last year's course, I found myself to be increasingly irritated. I found that concepts were being presented, but the handouts lacked a clarity of purpose. Therefore, I stepped back and I asked myself "What is it that I want students to know/learn from this chapter?" What material is important for them to grasp? I then proceeded to write down class outcomes for the upcoming class that I was to teach as a way to structure and inform me (and the students) as to the material that was relevant and that needed to be covered. (See Samples: The CPU and Memory Competencies)

Students are no doubt beneficiaries of the improved product that results in applying CBE to the teaching/learning process. In fact, a recent anecdotal example demonstrates how they may be even transformed by it. Recently, I was teaching a Computer Literacy course and one evening, near the end of class, a former student showed up presumably to give a ride home to an acquaintance. The former student observed the class exercise that her acquaintance was working on and started talking about her computer skills now. That she uses AOL to get on the Internet, that she uses email and instant messaging. The specific details are hazy now as I recount the story but I recall being struck by how much growth that I saw in her. A few semesters ago when she was taking my Computer Literacy course, this student seemed to struggle even to be overwhelmed at times. Now she was exuding a confidence in dealing with computers that was not quite present during the course. I would like to think that having my course put her on the path of computer literacy.

Although CBE has been described largely as an internal process, an internal focus does paradoxically tend to shift one's attention outward again. Following the "path" of CBE has improved my ability to be more responsive or attentive to the needs of students during class. How is that? Clearly articulating and understanding competencies for a lesson gives me the instructor more confidence in what I expect students to be able to do as a result of the lesson. The instructional content and techniques chosen for a given lesson flow from those clearly stated outcomes. By mastering these elements, it has a way of freeing the mind during a class to worry more about how the students are responding/doing than what I am doing. It has the benefit of shifting one's focus outward instead of being preoccupied inward. Hence, it helps create and foster a more developed ability of being student-centered. It has even lead in those rare occasions to a profound sense of "being in the moment." On occasion, students comment that "You make it seem so easy." Perhaps this is the case because what is produced in those exceptional moments are a product of the totality of one's gifts, not simply of the rational mind, but one's entire being.

Then finally there is the question of the working title, *The Zen of CBE: Implementing Competency Based Education in Higher Education*. This title occurred to me one evening when Eileen and I were discussing the book further after our official meeting with Barb had ended. We were trying to come up with an appropriate title. There was another working title but for me it did not capture the imagination of a prospective reader. Then, suddenly the title "The Zen of CBE" occurred to me. It was really the only title that I seriously considered as a possibility. However, the title was NOT a gimmick as one perusing a library or a bookstore might initially conclude. Instead the title was in a sense the confluence of two important parts to my life. Although that title changed, it continues to convey for me, the heart and soul of competency based education for reasons I discuss below.

In my college days I was drawn to eastern philosophy as a student of physics. The popular works *The Dancing Wu Li Masters* and *The Tao of Physics* were early influences. This was due no doubt to the deep respect that I had for science and its ability through theories to explain the workings of the universe. These works in particular left me intrigued because they showed the parallels between theories in modern physics and beliefs of eastern religions like Hinduism and Buddhism. I soon found myself devouring works from other eastern philosophy sources and authors, such as Alan Watts, *The Way of Zen*, and Joseph Campbell's *The Power of Myth*.

After leaving college, I eventually became employed teaching at the college level. That has been my daily routine for the past 10 years or so. After a few years of teaching, I first learned of CBE. I eventually zeroed in on the iterative nature/process of teaching as succinctly captured in the waterfall model. This was no doubt due in part to experience in engineering school with software development and project work that proceeded along an iterative process. So as I reflected on CBE and how I was experiencing it, I appreciated this process view.

Therefore, the working title of this book, *The Zen of CBE* was an outgrowth of the focus on what I was doing daily as a teacher, as illustrated by the waterfall model, and the instant recognition of this as similar to Zen Buddhism. Dormant in my consciousness was the image of Zen from the popular work *Zen and the Art of Motorcycle Maintenance*. The following passage describing the process of mountain climbing suggests this mental image of Zen.

> The ego-climber looks up the trail trying to see what's ahead even when he knows what's ahead because he just looked a second before. He goes too fast or too slow for the conditions and when he talks his talk is forever about somewhere else, something else. He's here but he's not here. He rejects the here, is unhappy with it, wants to be farther up the trail but when he gets there will be just as unhappy because then it will be "here." What he's looking for, what he wants, is all around him, but he doesn't want that because it is all around him. Every step's an effort, both physically and spiritually, because he imagines his goal to be external and distant.[37]

Zen, by contrast, does not emphasize the destination or the goal as the ego climber tends to. The image that one gets is of Zen as a journey as a process. To focus so intensely on the destination the goal means that there is no enjoyment in the present. To be so preoccupied with reaching the mountain summit means that

---

[37] Robert M. Pirsig, *Zen and the Art of Motorcycle Maintenance* (Toronto: Bantam Books, 1984) 189-190.

one may not stop and smell the flowers or enjoy the vistas in short enjoy the journey to the top.

The working title captured for me, in a deep sense, the harmony between these eastern philosophical teachings and the life lived out daily as a teacher. The essence of Zen is all about what happens in your everyday life. Being a teacher for me has come to mean in large part following the CBE process.

Therefore, before getting into the specifics of what was done in a given course, I felt it was important to understand the journey that I unwittingly began. The journey with CBE that I embarked upon has lead to a perceptual "transformation." So in a real sense that was also my connection to Zen. It has become a way of life in a sense, that being a teacher is not so much what you do but it becomes what you are. When you pour your energies and creativity into an endeavor it has a way over time of gradually changing you. I feel it has changed me for the better. I hope that following the CBE path may change you for the better also and your students will be the beneficiaries.

Implementing CBE in CIS

Computer Information Systems (CIS)/Information Technology Programs are increasingly being pressured by external agencies to reform their curriculum. For instance, the Association for Computing Machinery (ACM) has developed curriculum guidelines for Computer Science in 2001, Information Systems in 2002, and for Computer Engineering in 2004.[38] They are currently working on a draft of Information Technology guidelines[39]. All of these efforts are important developments if followed in steering/influencing college's to modify and change their program competencies and outcomes and to teach to them so that graduates are better able to be gainfully employed in the field.

For many years, the CIS Program at CCSJ has articulated program competencies. An example program outcome is "It is expected that students will

---

[38] Association of Computing Machinery, "ACM Curricula Recommendations," ACM: The First Society in Computing, 2005, 1 October 2005, http://www.acm.org/education/curricula.html>.

[39] Association of Computing Machinery.

For many years, the CIS Program at CCSJ has articulated program competencies. An example program outcome is "It is expected that students will demonstrate the ability to use a variety of computer applications, including telecommunications, word processing, desktop publishing, graphics, spreadsheet and data base programs to process information". If one "Googles" the keywords "computer technology competencies," one will uncover a myriad of technology competencies for various colleges and universities. Some of the outcomes are of a general nature, e.g. use computer applications, others are of ever increasing levels of specificity.

This perhaps leads to my bias/orientation towards CBE. I have always felt that general technology outcomes although necessary, are almost too limiting to be of substantial value. For instance, what does it mean to "use computer applications?" What should students be able to do with them? My idea of what is fundamental use of a computer application may differ from yours. Hence, I have had a natural gravitation towards the more detailed competencies that are usually more appropriately stated at the course and class level then at the program level. Because for me, this extra detail goes a long way in removing the ambiguity inherent in general program competencies.

My belief has been that a program any program consists of the building blocks of its courses and a course consists of the building blocks of its classes. Therefore, it is only ultimately at the class level and then the course level that the program competencies whatever they may be are actually realized. These two notions have helped lead me to embrace the pedagogical approach to CBE as represented in the waterfall or iterative model. This approach focuses on what happens in a course and what happens in a class. Because it is only in the classroom with actual students that theory by necessity meets practice.

Implementing CBE in Computer Literacy

Introduction

Computer literacy at CCSJ is a three credit hour required course that is part of the general education program. The course is housed in the CIS program but was designed to be delivered exclusively with the goal of meeting the general computer proficiency needs throughout the college.

The Curriculum

The curriculum includes both computer concepts and computer applications. Describing it another way, it covers both hardware and software literacy. Hardware literacy means the knowledge of computer hardware and terminology that is useful to someone who has purchased or intends to purchase a computer and/or someone who needs to interact with technical support staff to resolve a computer problem. Software literacy largely means an ability to use a computer and computer applications. The software and software concepts include word processing, presentation graphics, spreadsheets, WWW browsers and Internet searching, and file management.

The curriculum is delivered via some lecture and instructor demonstrations, collaborative learning exercises/class exercises (formative assessments), and summative assessments that include true/false and multiple choice sections (for the knowledge based aspects) and performance-based assessments. These performance-based assessments are "hands-on" exercises that are completed by the student without any assistance from other students or the instructor.

The use of technology is a key feature in many CIS courses, including the computer literacy course. For instance, the judicious use of technology has been a factor in facilitating students' learning. Software application demonstrations are performed in the instructional computer lab making use of software like NetMeeting and NetSupport to project the instructor's station to the students' monitors. The practice has been to schedule classes in CIS with a heavy lab component directly in one of the instructional labs to allow this possibility. This was also due to the lack of "smart classrooms" until recently. The newer NetSupport software has the advantage that it allows the instructor to display the Windows Desktop, a capability that the older NetMeeting did not have; it was limited in that it could only display a window. Another downside to NetMeeting usage was that the students had to actively join the instructor-initiated conference by double-clicking an icon. For users with a limited computer background the extra steps tended to be problematic.

The NetSupport software also allows an instructor to maintain more control in the process. NetSupport features a "scan" mode where the instructor can view what students are doing at their workstations and even take control to explain something. This has been somewhat useful in an open lab setting.

Another practice is to introduce students to the college's e-learning environment, Blackboard. In this course, student are given Blackboard accounts and shown how to log in and log out. They are also introduced to some of the communication features such as the Discussion Board. The intent is to merely expose them to the environment so that they will be able to more easily use it in their other courses at CCSJ when the time comes.

Camtasia software is a software application that has been successfully used to create AVI tutorials. These AVI tutorials were first created to accompany a lab manual that was being developed for the course. These tutorials have been very helpful in the circumstance where a student misses a class, yet is then able to view the missed lesson on a recorded AVI tutorial after some initial instruction on how to use an AVI player (e.g. Windows Media Player, RealPlayer, or now Camtasia Player). It is also useful in situations where a motivated student has wanted to view a tutorial on a historically difficult topic (like file management) multiple times. Some experiments have been done to convert the AVI tutorials to streaming media versions and to incorporate such content onto Blackboard (for possible distance learning applications). The newer versions of Camtasia have allowed the straightforward creation of a CD menu that serves as a front-end to the AVI tutorials. This CD menu when burned to a CD will "autorun" (i.e. automatically start up) when the disc is inserted into the CD-ROM drive. This has the advantage of eliminating the obstacle of locating and starting up the correct file.

The competencies evolved and developed more as an outgrowth of the content creation process rather than being explicitly enumerated at the outset. They of course stemmed from my experience working in PC support and training settings both professional and personal. A considerable amount of thought was given to what should the student be able to do. Then, content and topics were selected with this end product in mind. After this was established, only later were the more detailed competencies that are now found on the course syllabus (See Samples: Computer Literacy - General Competencies) actually articulated. Although this may not be an ideal process, I think it does speak to the richness of the iterative/waterfall model of CBE. That the important thing is to get started in the process, then gradually you will experience the transformative effects that the process entails. Then shortly afterwards, the detailed weekly outcomes (See Samples: Computer Literacy – Detailed Competencies) were developed to articulate what was already being covered in the content side. This was intended to augment student learning by more clearly communicating to the student what the expectations would be on the eventual summative assessments.

Challenges

One area of challenge in the seemingly ever-changing field of computers is content creation and/or textbook selection. Earlier versions of the course used textbooks placing a heavier emphasis on computer concepts and theory. This necessitated the development of course handouts to cover the vital application/laboratory component. Eventually over time, these course handouts were packaged together into a single lab manual that was given to the students on the first class session. Gradually, there was a shift to a more application centric/"hands-on" approach. This resulted in a change in the course textbooks to ones that were more application driven. However, this has not decreased the necessity or the desire to use course handouts for those areas that are still poorly treated in the existing textbooks or the use of handouts to summarize the salient/important features in the material that is covered.

Another related point is the constant rapid pace of change in software versions. This necessitates the need to verify that application specific textbooks are chosen so that they will be in synchronization with the software that the school has licensed in the instructional labs. Also, the rapid changes in software versions can quickly outdate (at least to some extent) the custom course content that is created.

Another challenge has been the time consuming nature of the evaluation process, namely the performance-based assessments. Currently, the procedure is that at the beginning of the assessment, the student is given a test disk and a set of directions to perform. The test disk contains any files that are used as a starting point for the assessment and the student is expected to save all files to the test disk. The instructor when scoring the assessment inserts the student's test disk and then opens up the relevant files. The instructor then systematically checks point by point to see which operations were performed and how completely. The advantage to this approach is that it allows the discovery of errors that may be difficult or impossible to detect from a hard-copy only system. For example, a student in Microsoft Word would be committing a grave error by not letting paragraph text word wrap. However, a student could instead type paragraphs by hitting the return key at the end of every line, then undoing the automatic capitalization on the subsequent new line if required. This fact could potentially be concealed unless the file is actually opened and viewed with the non-printing symbols enabled. Another serious error would be a student in PowerPoint using 5 separate files for a 5 slide presentation. This type of error might not show up if one where to only look at the hardcopies of the slides. Of course, it would be very difficult to give an effective presentation if your presentation consisted of 5 files with one slide in each.

Currently, a point-based rubric is employed in grading the performance-based assessments. A point value is assigned to each subtask based on the perceived level of difficulty. Perhaps development of better rubrics might improve the grading efficiency somewhat. Perhaps gravitating toward specialized skills assessment software that some computer book publishers now offer could eliminate much of the drudgery involved in this sort of detailed grading. Historically, the problem with this type of software has been its inflexibility. In early versions, users tended to need to perform an operation in a specific manner. For instance, if the competency is to bold text, then the user would need to do so say by clicking the bold icon on the toolbar to be credited by the software. If the user used a keyboard shortcut, a CTRL+b in this case, then the software would not recognize this as a valid method even though it is a perfectly legitimate method.

Another challenge has been that the course can combine users with disparate skill levels. Since the course is a required part of General Education, it can sometimes combine users with little or no computer experience with users who are quite computer literate. In addition, since there is only one course dedicated to computer skills in the General Education curriculum, there can be a tendency for the instructor to try to force as much content as possible since it is deemed needed and necessary. This can leave a student that enters the course with little or no computer skills overwhelmed.

There are alternative models that could be employed. A computer literacy proficiency test could be offered to students as an alternative to taking the computer literacy course. There have been some problems to date with the development of such a test. For one, there needs to be consensus on what such a test should contain. Should the test be a basic computer literacy test or a computer literacy test that more closely reflects the content covered in the computer literacy course? A two-person computer competency task force, at one point, was established to develop computer competencies presumably for such an eventual test. The task force met and developed an action plan to start first with developing detailed hardware and software competencies for such a test. Then, we planned to tackle the issue of designing such an assessment based on the competencies developed. The task force did succeed in developing more detailed hardware competencies. This had always been an area where the competencies for the computer literacy course were lacking. However, due to employee turnover, the effort became stalled. Another potential obstacle is the required institutional resources and manpower to administer such a system. There is also the pragmatic concern in the CIS program of the negative impact to credit-hour production.

Another challenge has been a student's receptivity to new learning and the problem of unlearning bad habits. Sometimes a student's initial mindset is that he knows everything that he needs to know about computers or worse yet he needs to unlearn ingrained bad habits that were formed as a result of trial and error without any formal or proper computer instruction. A common example is with file management. Some students will think, "Why do I need to know how to do this?" It is only after a number of months or years of working with a computer and accumulating the concomitant number of files that one wishes they could find what they are looking for and hence finally appreciates the need to create folders to organize their work.

One area where experience teaching has produced a significant shift in my thinking is in appreciating the importance of the affective domain of learning. As a student, I tended to be receptive and willing to learn. I tended not to question the instructor's judgment on why we were learning something. I suppose it was that I had a basic faith in teachers initially until or unless proven otherwise. When teaching my students, I discovered that they did not necessarily share all my attitudes and beliefs. Some students displayed a great fear of computers. Some resisted performing certain computer related tasks. Some students even questioned or doubted the utility of what material was being presented. Having a commitment to the CBE learning process allowed me to gradually narrow in on this source of difficulty and to implement strategies to overcome it. Now, I make a more concerted effort to actively combat these attitudes. I try to gradually encourage students so that their fear will gradually diminish. I have learned to be on the lookout for opportunities where a student might question what we are doing and to be prepared to give a motivation or explanation of why this knowledge or skill is useful and/or important to know. Whereas earlier in my teaching career, I tended to focus more on the mechanics of whatever technique was in the lesson plan (e.g. build a spreadsheet).

Samples

The CPU and Memory Competencies

- Recognize the components of a real CPU in the Little Man Computer (LMC)
- Describe a CPU register
- Describe the purpose of the CPU registers: accumulator, program counter, instruction register, memory address register, memory data or buffer register
- List the four primary types of register operations
- Describe the organization and operation of computer memory
- Understand the factors that determine the capacity of memory in a real computer
- State the various types of computer memory implementations including their purpose and their technological advantages and disadvantages
- Draw a simplified block-diagram of the CPU and memory systems
- Illustrate the fetch-execute cycle for the LMC instructions in terms of register operations
- Define the purpose of a bus
- Understand the factors that contribute to bus performance
- Recognize the architectural components of a modern motherboard
- Produce specifications for a customized computer system using "bare" hardware components

Computer Literacy - General Competencies

Students in this course will:

- **Identify the major components of a computer and their functions**
- **Use a personal computer and its Graphical User Interface (GUI) effectively**
  - initiate and terminate a computer work session (e.g. "powering-on" a computer, successfully logging into a computer network, and shutting down a computer)

- o   manage the desktop (e.g. starting and exiting application programs, manipulating windows)
- o   multitask (e.g. switch between multiple concurrent application programs, transfer information between two documents and/or applications)

- **Use word processing software at a basic-level mastery including**
  - o   use a computer keyboard to enter text into a document
  - o   use the appropriate commands to edit text (e.g. add new text to an existing document, delete text, move text)
  - o   apply and remove basic formatting (e.g. change margins, line spacing, character formatting)
  - o   produce a hard copy of a document

- **Use presentation graphics software at a basic-level mastery including**
  - o   create a bulleted list presentation from an outline
  - o   edit a slide presentation (e.g. add new slides, edit slide text, delete slides, reorder or reposition slides) as needed
  - o   work with graphics, including inserting clipart or other graphic formats, resizing and repositioning images
  - o   animate presentation text and/or graphics
  - o   use the appropriate navigation controls to mechanically deliver a slide show
  - o   generate the appropriate hard copy printouts (i.e. presentation slides for the speaker and handouts for the audience)

- **Use spreadsheet software at a basic-level mastery including**
  - o   enter text and numbers into a given spreadsheet cell
  - o   create spreadsheet formulas combining the appropriate mathematical formulas and/or built-in functions and the appropriate cell references.
  - o   apply and remove simple cell formatting (e.g. number styles, character formatting styles)
  - o   produce a hard copy of a spreadsheet

- **Use a WWW browser effectively**
  - o   construct the appropriate URL using the WWW naming conventions (i.e. guess the correct URL)
  - o   display a web page given a specific URL
  - o   issue the commands to follow a graphical or textual hyperlink
  - o   use the browser's navigation controls to efficiently navigate
  - o   save a given URL for future reference

- **Use the Internet effectively as a source of information**
  - o   select the appropriate keywords for an Internet search given a problem statement

- o　　　use a search engine efficiently by performing advanced queries (e.g. Boolean AND searches and exact quote searches)
- o　　　use the appropriate WWW browser commands to efficiently search for a keyword(s) in a lengthy multi-page document (e.g. Find in Page feature)
- o　　　use the appropriate WWW browser commands to print a small select number of pages in a lengthy multi-page document (e.g. Print Preview and Print commands)

- **Perform common file management tasks**
- o　　　work with files during a single computer work session and over multiple work sessions
- o　　　display a storage device's hierarchical folder/directory structure and then navigate to a specific drive/folder and display the contents
- o　　　create a given folder/directory structure on a 3.5" floppy disk
- o　　　manipulate files and folders (e.g. copy files from an arbitrary drive/folder to an arbitrary drive folder, rename a given folder and/or file, delete a given file and/or folder)
- o　　　erase and format a floppy disk as required

- **Use electronic forms of communication**
- o　　　create, send, and retrieve electronic mail
- o　　　recognize a valid Internet e-mail address
- o　　　create an e-mail message including both the message body and the subject line
- o　　　send a given e-mail to a single recipient and/or to multiple recipients
- o　　　send an e-mail attachment (e.g. word processed document, JPEG image)
- o　　　use newsgroups/bulletin board systems (e.g. create messages, post and reply to messages)

Computer Literacy – Week #1 Detailed Competencies

- Know the two simple definitions of "what is a computer"
- Know simple definitions for computer hardware and computer software
- Be familiar with the hardware components of a computer (i.e. identify the hardware from a picture or a model; know what the function/purpose of the hardware is; if there are multiple types of a particular hardware device, then understand the types of technologies used, their advantages and disadvantages, etc.)
  - o System Unit
  - o CPU
  - o RAM
  - o Input Devices (keyboard, mouse, etc)

- o Output Devices (monitor, printers, etc)
- o Storage Devices (floppy disk, hard disk, optical disks, etc)
- Understand the purpose/function of the Operating System
- Understand the purpose of Application Software
- Be able to perform the following tasks <u>without</u> any assistance except perhaps a quick reference to your notes or textbooks
  - o Be able to power on a CCSJ computer
  - o Be able to successfully log-in to the CCSJ network
  - o Know the two simple tests that verify your login was most likely successful
  - o Be able to identify the following Windows 9x screen elements: Desktop, Task Bar, Desktop Icons, Start Button, Start Button Menus, Quick Launch Toolbar, Tray Area, Taskbar buttons
  - o Be comfortable using a mouse in the Windows 9x GUI
    - ▪ Be able to perform/describe the mouse operations: point, click, double-click, and drag
  - o Be able to start an application from the Desktop, from the Quick Launch Toolbar, and/or from the Start Menu.
  - o Be able to identify the following window screen elements: title bar, window border, minimize, maximize/restore, close buttons, etc.
  - o Be able to perform/describe the following window operations
    - ▪ Resize a window
    - ▪ Reposition a window
    - ▪ Minimize and Redisplay a window
    - ▪ Maximize and Restore a window
    - ▪ Close a window
  - o Be able to <u>properly</u> power down a computer

Computer Literacy – Week #2 Detailed Competencies

Microsoft Word and the MLA Format

- Be able to open a Word document from a given folder on the "Network drive"
- Be able to use the Save As operation to save a document on the network drive to a portable storage device
- Be able to switch between the "Normal" view, the "Print Layout", and the "Header and Footer" view as needed
- Be able to hide and display the "Ruler"
- Be able to associate the appropriate screen element on the Ruler with the first-line indent, left indent, and hanging indent operations
- Understand the difference between indents and margins
- Be able to set the document's margins
- Be able to double-space a paragraph or multiple paragraphs

- Be able to first-line indent a paragraph or multiple paragraphs
- Be able to remove paragraph formatting or change the paragraph formatting back to the default settings
- Be able to create a header
- Be able to insert the proper page code to number the pages
- Be able to insert a manual page break at the desired point in a document
- Be able to delete a page break if needed
- Be able to properly format the "Works Cited" references in the hanging indent format
- Be able to use Word's Print Preview feature
- Be able to use Word's Word Count feature if needed

Computer Literacy – Week #4 Detailed Competencies

Windows XP – Project 3

- Be able to start the My Computer/Windows Explorer application
- Be able to understand the purpose of the right pane and the left pane in the Windows Explorer application window
- Be able to associate a storage device with the appropriate drive letter in Windows XP
- Be able to view an object's properties (e.g. file or drive)
  - o Be able to view the amount of used and free space available on a storage device
- Be able to understand the purpose/function of a folder
- Be able to expand and contract a drive's folder/directory structure
- Be able to understand the concept of a path
- Be able to create a given folder/directory structure on a storage device (e.g. 3 ½" floppy disk)
- Be able to view or display the contents of a given folder
- Be able to recognize the associated application from a file's icon displayed in Windows Explorer or alternatively from a file's extension
- Be able to change the default view of a folder's contents (e.g. Icons, List, Details)
- Be able to sort a folder's content by type (i.e. extension) and by filename when using the Details view
- Be able to rename a file or folder (as needed)
- Be able to select multiple files using the ctrl + clicking technique
- Be able to copy (and move) files from a given drive/folder to a given drive/folder
- Be able to delete files and folders (as needed)
- Be able to exit or close the Windows Explorer application
- Be able to work with the Recycle Bin

100

- o View the Recycle Bin contents
- o Restore selected items from the Recycle Bin
- o Delete selected items from the Recycle Bin
- o Empty the entire contents of the Recycle Bin
- Be able to virus scan a floppy disk in the CCSJ labs

Computer Literacy – Week #6 Detailed Competencies

Internet Explorer (IE) – Project 1

- Be able to understand the structure of the World Wide Web (WWW) as an interconnected collection of hypertext documents
- Be familiar with the general form of a WWW URL
- Be familiar with the common top level domains
- Be able to start the Internet Explorer application
- Be able to use the Address Bar to navigate to a specific URL
- Be able to use a knowledge of Internet naming conventions to guess a URL
- Be able to use a mouse to follow text and graphic links
- Be able to scroll the IE's display area to view long Web pages
- Be able to navigate backward and forward (i.e. using the Back and Forward Toolbar buttons or the Back and Forward menu items on the shortcut menu) to a desired page
- Be able to understand the use of the Stop and Refresh buttons
- Be able to save a URL for future reference (e.g. use IE's Favorites feature or create a Desktop shortcut)
- Be able to save a picture (e.g. JPG image) from a Web page
- Be able to use the Print Preview feature
  - o Be able to Zoom In and Zoom Out as needed
  - o Be able to move forward and move backward as needed
- Be able to print a hard copy of a Web page
  - o Be able to print the entire print range
  - o Be able to print a subset of the entire print range
    - Use the Find feature to locate a specific word in a long web document
    - Use the Print Preview feature to locate which range of pages to print
- Be able to exit the Internet Explorer application

Computer Literacy – Week #7 Detailed Competencies

Internet Explorer (IE) – Project 2

- Be able to evaluate a Web page according to the criteria of its authorship, accuracy of information, currency of information, and topic and scope of coverage

- Be familiar with several different search engine WWW sites
- Be able to use an Internet directory to retrieve information on a desired topic or subject
- Be able to use a search engine
  - Be familiar with the common successful search strategies
    - Be able to select relevant and useful keywords from a problem statement
    - Be able to refine the keywords based on the results of a keyword search
    - Be familiar with the use of a search engine's inclusion or exclusion capability to help narrow a search
    - Be familiar with the purpose of a wildcard
  - Be able to perform simple keyword searches
  - Be able to perform compound condition searches using the Boolean AND operator
  - Be able to perform exact quote searches
- Be able to use a browser's Find feature to quickly locate a keyword or keywords on a lengthy Web page document

CIS 115 – Computer Literacy

Week #11

Excel Class Exercise

Problem: Your favorite professor has asked your assistance in preparing a spreadsheet to determine the costs of graduation garments (academic regalia). She would like to see a cost breakdown of the types of doctoral garments. The academic regalia consists of a **gown**, a **hood**, a mortarboard **cap**, and a **tassel**. Jostens, the college's supplier, makes three styles of doctoral gowns: *Devon, Sussex,* and *Windsor*. The costs in the order listed are $225, $300, and $475. The doctoral hood, cap and tassel costs are fixed for the three different styles. These costs are $75 for the hood, $15.50 for the cap, and $2 for the tassel. Before leaving her office, she remembers that the college has offered to defray $125 of the total costs, so she would like this included in the spreadsheet as well.

1. After a little thought on the problem, you decide to layout the spreadsheet as follows:

	Devon	Sussex	Windsor
Gown	$ XXX.XX	$ XXX.XX	$ XXX.XX
Hood	XX.XX	XX.XX	XX.XX
Cap	XX.XX	XX.XX	XX.XX
Tassel	X.XX	X.XX	X.XX
Subtotal	$ XXX.XX	$ XXX.XX	$ XXX.XX
College Discount	XXX.XX	XXX.XX	XXX.XX
Grand Total	$ XXX.XX	$ XXX.XX	$ XXX.XX

2. Start Microsoft Excel and create the spreadsheet shown above. Be sure to create formulas for the Subtotal and Totals rows. Remember to subtract the college discount to arrive at the grand total.

3. Underline, italicize, and bold the text cells as shown. Format the numbers using the comma style and the accounting style with 2 decimal places as shown. Add a single bottom border under the subtotal cells and a double bottom border under the grand total cells as shown above. Manually resize the columns to the approximate sizes shown above.

4. Print a hardcopy of the spreadsheet to take to your professor. Be sure to use print preview first however to catch the condition of the spreadsheet overflow onto two pages.

5. Exit Microsoft Excel when you are completed.

104

CIS 115 Excel Assessment Checklist/Rubric

(<u>Directions</u>: Place a check mark v or an X next to each item)

<u>Spreadsheet Layout</u>

_____ Avoided blank columns and/or rows between spreadsheet items

<u>Program Start and Exit/Program Output</u>

_____ Able to start the application program using a desktop icon or using the Start Programs folder

_____ Able to produce a hardcopy of the spreadsheet in question

_____ Able to exit the application program (with or without saving the file)

<u>Data Entry/Formulas</u>

_____ Able to accurately type the spreadsheet items (i.e. text, data, and formulas) including using the proper case and spelling

_____ Used formulas (either a) addition operators with the proper cell references or b) sum function with a proper range) in the subtotal row

_____ Used formulas for the grand total row including a subtraction operator with the proper cell references

_____ Used formulas for the grand total row including a subtraction operator with the proper cell reference

_____ Showed evidence of using a formula copy operation as opposed to individual formula creation

<u>Formatting</u>

_____ Able to properly format (i.e. underline, bold, and italicize) the text cells

_____ Able to properly format (i.e. accounting and/or comma style, 2 decimal digits) the number cells

_____ Able to recognize and apply cell alignments (right and left)

_____ Able to apply the desired bottom borders (single and double) to the appropriate cells

_____ Able to manually resize columns

_____ Showed evidence of selecting cell ranges before applying formatting

Chapter 4

Implementing Competency Based Education in Clinical and Social Services Education

Eileen Stenzel

> Competency-based education sets before itself a set of observable, desired outcomes. These outcomes serve primarily as a form of communication. For the students, the declared outcomes represent notification of the return they should expect for their tuition and effort. For the teachers, the outcomes provide a basis for the selection of content and the organization of its delivery. For the institution, the expressed outcomes represent an operational definition of its mission statement.[40]

Implementing CBE in programs of professional studies has a valuable resource in the literature of professional organizations, certifying agencies and state boards of professional regulation that issue the professional license. This literature conveys the current consensus of the profession as to what entry level professionals should know and know how to do upon completion of the undergraduate and graduate degrees.

The Human Services Programs draws on the competencies identified by the Council for Standards in Human Service Education (CSHSE) and the National

---

[40] George Kuehn, Personal Interview, 15 July 2000.

Organization for Human Services (NOHS).[41] These competencies provide the framework for the development of a Curriculum Map that, in turn, guides the process of writing course syllabi. The course syllabi present the specific learning objectives that will move students toward mastery of the competencies for which that course is responsible in the overall curriculum.

The backward design of a program curriculum is one of the most essential characteristics of CBE. It is, therefore, a defining element in the implementation of CBE in existing and new programs. The purpose of the professional curriculum is to prepare students to function as competent professionals who know how to continue to advance their knowledge and skills. This goal is achieved step by step, course by course as students expand the knowledge and skills and enhance their ability to apply these skills to problems they will encounter in their chosen profession. Professional standards identify the long term goals of any program of professional education. Program objectives reflect these standards. Course objectives specify how these program objectives will be achieved and assessed.

With this "backward design" model in place , the Human Services Program developed guidelines for implementing CBE in its curriculum. The guidelines are being developed using the understanding of CBE and The Taxonomy presented above. They will be distributed to all full and part-time HSV teaching personnel and shared with the faculty-at-large. They will be used to assess the current level of practice characteristic of each of these programs, identify where the program is demonstrating consistency with CBE and how CBE can strengthen aspects of the programs that are less consistent with CBE.

1. **Explicitly state the knowledge, skills and attitudes that the HSV student should have mastered upon completion of the**

---

[41] Cf. Howard S. Harris and David Maloney, eds., *Human Services* (Boston: Allyn and Bacon, 1999)113ff.

HSV programs. In CBE, curriculum design is backward: it begins with clearly stated professional outcomes from which program objectives are identified. Courses are designed in relation to these program objectives. Each class unit in a specific course moves toward attainment of knowledge and skills essential to mastering course objectives.

Strategy 1: The Curriculum Map will state the knowledge, skills and attitude sets in specific, measurable terms. This map is part of the resource material for the Introductory courses.

Strategy 2: The knowledge, skills and attitudes developed in each course in the curriculum are clearly stated in course syllabi and at the beginning of each instructional unit.

Examples in the Cognitive Domain:

Knowledge/Understanding Base: Students will be able to identify and explain the components of an effective interview for information sharing purposes.

Application: Students will demonstrate the ability to conduct an interview intended to inform clients about the risk factors for contracting HIV/AIDS/ STD'S

Example in the Affective Domain:

Set: Through simulation exercises students will demonstrate a nonjudgmental set of attitudes toward persons at risk for contracting HIV/AIDS/STDS.

2.   **Maximize the transfer of knowledge, skills and values to the workplace setting.**   The practice and assessment of knowledge, skills and values necessary for an effective HSV professional should take the same form as the workplace. That is, instruction and assessment should be designed to be consistent with desired outcomes and simulate real world of work challenges.

Reading about or knowing about procedures and skills is not the same as being able to perform them well.

It is important that assessment activities reflect the form as the desired outcome. For example, if interviewing for data collection purposes is an important skill for the HSV then assessment should include the actual or simulated demonstration of this skill. Paper and pencil assessments tend to evaluate a student's knowledge about and/or understanding of a skill and even his./her ability to analyze and critique. Paper and pencil assessments tend not to evaluate the students ability to apply what he/she has learned. Moreover, over reliance on paper and pencil tests reflect the influence of language and reading skills rather than the students ability to engage in a specific procedure. Or set of procedures.

3. **Use data to support procedural learning**. The HSV programs are applied social and behavioral science disciplines. Most students will come into the program with a pattern of thinking that is characteristically judgmental and moralistic. Our job is to help them think like social and behavioral scientists, i.e. their task is to understand behavior, help people expand their options and make choices that they deem to be in their best interest. The HSV professional must be able to draw conclusions based on what the data support and implement intervention strategies that have a reasonable probability of success.

4. **CBE is motivated by long-term objectives**. At every point instructors should be able to answer the question, "What is it that I want these students to know and know how to do when this class, course, program ends?" Instructors need to be effective at conveying these outcomes to students throughout the program to aid the student's developing investment in those same outcomes as

one strategy toward helping student complete the program(s) through the development of professional identity.

5.   **Select instructional materials that support instructional methods.** For example, in the Introductory courses, students might be asked to formulate an initial position on general principles that should inform the delivery of health care in this country. This complex task requires that the issue be broken down into its various components and that students be thoroughly engaged at each level of the discussion. Specifically, students will need direct instruction and supervised practice in listening to various positions, simulation exercises that require them to formulate and express several different points of view as if each view represented the one that they affirmed, debating from various points of view and then formulating a position. For learning outcomes that are more procedural in nature the same principle applies. Student should receive direct instruction in which learning outcomes are identified, opportunities to observe demonstration of the skills, supervised practice of those skills, and finally, independent performance of the skills.

Example: students may be expected to engage in prenatal health education. Instructors must be able to define what it is that students need to know and know how to do to be effective in this task. Instructional environments are designed "backward", i.e. designed starting with this endpoint and an analysis of what it will take to help students master this knowledge and skill set.

6.   **Procedural outcomes require both supervised and independent practice for mastery.** Example: Referral and follow-up skills.

1. Instructors would identify the elements of effective referral and follow-up.

2. Instructors will demonstrate referral and follow-up procedures using simulated cases.

3. Students will participate in simulated exercises to demonstrate referral and follow-up procedures.

4. Students will be assigned a series of mock interviews to be recorded using audio and/or video tape. The interviews will be evaluated by the instructors using pre-determined criteria that have been distributed to students as part of the instructional process.[42]

In addition to these guidelines, a Checklist is being used to evaluate current HSV and syllabi for compliance with CBE.

Section One Summary

CBE requires clearly stated behavioral objectives, instructional activities designed around these objectives and the use of formative and summative assessment procedures to support maximum attainment of these learning goals. The biggest barriers to the initial implementation of CBE are: 1) the failure to develop observable, measurable objectives, 2) over reliance on summative assessment and 3) disconnected objectives, instructional activities and assessment.

By using The Taxonomy to formulate observable, measurable objectives, instructors and students alike are able to identify what kinds of activities (i.e. competencies) represent each level of learning. This type of clarity and specification of outcomes is the basis for designing a) instructional activities that

---

[42] Cf. "Suggestions for Effective Railroad Tank Car Loading/Unloading Training Programs: Instructional Methods," *Publication of Federal Railroad Administration Office of Research and Development* (N.p.: Publication of Federal Railroad Administration Office of Research and Development, 1999) Google, 1 July 2000 <http://www.fra.dot.gov/downloads/safety/sertcl2.pdf>.

are intended to help students master those competencies and b) assessment tools that do, in fact, measure the degree to which students are progressing toward and attaining mastery of those competencies.

Section Two: Issues and Concerns Unique to the Higher Education Environment

There are three issues unique to the higher education setting that impact the implementation of Competency Based Education. First, Colleges and universities, especially small, private tuition-driven institutions, will always struggle with shifting markets and changing expectations about the marketability of the undergraduate degree. Second, CBE originated in training programs in business and industry settings. Because of this focus on training CBE is suspect among college and university faculty who insist, and rightly so, that higher education must always be about more than training. Third, College and University faculty are increasingly being challenged to respond to the impact of "the information age" on preparing professionals for the 21st Century. The rate at which new information is disseminated requires an emphasis in professional education that includes not only preparation to enter the profession but also development of the ability to lead the profession. Teachers, social workers, business managers, health care providers and managers of heath care systems will all need to know about their profession to enter it well. But they will also need to be able to assess the implications of new information, changing social and political settings and shifting expectations of client/consumer populations to help their professions change and adapt to maintain and increase effectiveness. Colleges and universities are challenged, as they always have been, to focus curriculum, instruction and assessment on the development of these broad competencies. These three issues: the marketability of the degree as a factor in the survival of the institution, the need to understand CBE in terms of higher level learning, and, the impact of the rate at which new information is discovered and disseminated, create the challenge to design programs in professional education that that produce individuals who are able to use what they learn to perform the job as it currently exists and expand the job to meet new challenges. This image of the "reflective professional" conveys the well-grounded, adaptable individual who is able to respond in an innovative way to the changing demands of his/her profession as it is now and as it will unfold in the future.[43]

The importance of higher order thinking skills reflects a value deep in the traditions of higher education. Therefore, achieving the goal of producing reflective professionals for the 21st century is a challenge from the future that is at once compatible with a most cherished tradition of higher education: producing thoughtful, well-informed reflective, competent graduates. Competency Based Education is an approach to higher education that focuses specific attention on mastery of higher level learning skills. Additionally, CBE emphasizes the importance of opportunities for students to master the *integration* of various bodies of knowledge and skills into the problem-solving process. While a program curriculum can easily divide the aspects of a job in the world into specific courses of study, the reality of professional life is more complicated. Most challenges professionals face require them to draw *simultaneously* on different bodies of knowledge and skill for effective problem-solving and change management. The type of professional education these challenges demand is consistent with the most valued traditions of higher education: the development of higher order skills. Far from being an opponent of higher level learning, CBE is, in fact, a tool for strengthening the attaining higher-level outcomes with students.

There always has been and always will be a place for knowledge based courses in the college curriculum. These courses serve important functions. They broaden students' awareness of the world around them and the people in it. They inspire new curiosities and a sense of wonder. And, they challenge students to study areas that they might not otherwise pursue. Nevertheless, the primary

---

[43] See the discussion of the planning model in Chapter One.

function of the undergraduate curriculum is now as it always has been: to prepare students be competent, purposeful and ethical in their personal and professional lives. To achieve this goal students master the processes of getting information and knowing what to do with it once they get it. Given the rapid rate at which new information becomes available, no program can claim to teach students *everything* they will need to know or know how to do to function in the professional environments of their choice. More than anything else, the information age as redefined the nature of professional work, what it means to stay current and employ standards of best practice. As the reality of the 21st Century Professional adapts to the information age so, too, must programs of professional education. In both undergraduate and graduate programs students must complete their degrees ready to function effectively in the world of work. They must be experienced at integrating new learning into established foundations. They must be able to re-evaluate old ideas and generate new and innovative methods for responding to the challenges of their profession. In the CBE model of curriculum design this means that consistent attention must be given to providing opportunities for students to learn how to transfer what they are learning to problems they will encounter in the workplace in a format that requires them respond to ever increasingly difficult problems and integrate an ever-broadening body of knowledge and skills. Using The Taxonomy it is clear to see that what will most characterize the 21st Century Professional is mastery of upper level learning skills. Competency Based Education *does not question* the importance of these objectives. What CBE does propose is that *whatever the desired outcome,* that outcome needs to be:

1.   stated in measurable, observable terms;
2.   identified for students at the outset of instruction;
3.   demonstrated repeatedly;
4.   practice repeatedly with supervision and instructional interventions to improve performance; and.

5.   assessed for mastery.

These characteristics of CBE challenge the "information in-put; behavior out-put" assumptions of more traditional approaches to higher education. The conflict is less about values and more about *methodology*. This focus on methodology is frequently discussed in terms of an over reliance on the lecture method by college and university professors. The issue, however, has less to do with the lecture method and more to do with an instructor's ability to:

1.   design instructional units that engage students in active learning;

2.   use formative assessment procedures as an instructional tool to *verify* what students are doing with the information they are encountering;

3.   make instructional changes where needed; and,

4.   offer meaningful feedback to students as they progress toward the development of the expected competencies.

Lectures that are designed around attainment of higher order thinking can, in fact, be an effective instructional tool provided they are not the only tool.

In addition to this debate about the lecture method, CBE and more traditional approaches to higher education have a somewhat different perspective on knowledge based learning. CBE does *not* reject knowledge based learning out of hand or dictate what outcomes instruction should pursue. CBE does, however, insist that knowledge based learning is *not sufficient* in professional education because of the importance of the transferability of academic skills to the workplace as a measure of effective professional education. More traditional approaches to higher education assume that if students are given a sufficiently broad exposure to what they need to know they will be able to transfer those skills to other settings. CBE rejects this assumption and insists that transferring knowledge and skills from one setting to another is an acquired skill that needs to be an integral part of any educational program. The CBE challenge to the over-reliance on the lecture method discussed above less a concern about method and more a concern about what kinds of methods support the attainment of higher order thinking skills. The bias of CBE is *not* with any one teaching method. The CBE bias is with the importance of the mastery of competencies as measured by the student's ability to apply them in the work place.[44]

Because CBE is an instructional design process that stresses the importance of operationalizing the language of outcomes it is a valuable resource for assisting college and university faculty efforts to help students attain the higher levels of learning so valued in higher education and so critical in effective professional education. These are: critical thinking, problem solving, freedom from institutional constraint in the pursuit of knowledge, and innovation.

Traditional approaches to higher education rely heavily on students' abilities at the time they enter college. The instructor's job is to offer an experience to the student. The student's job is to do something with that experience. Assessment is the instructor's evaluation of what the student did. By contract, CBE recognizes that some student's do, in fact, enter college from high school programs that equipped them with higher level learning skills. These students will attain higher levels of learning regardless of the instructional environment. However, CBE rests its case on three simple facts. First, even those best and brightest students acquired those skills. Second, those students do not, in fact, make up the majority of those enrolled in college, especially commuter colleges serving an adult population. CEB allows college faculty to level the playing field for those college students who got left behind by inferior elementary and secondary programs and now struggle to complete a college degree. CBE is an approach to instructional design, pedagogy and assessment that responds to the needs of those students who are especially dependent on the quality of instruction for educational attainment. CBE claims that the clearer

---

[44] Kerka.

teachers and students are about these outcomes and the more carefully instructional activities challenge students to perform them, the greater the likelihood that those competencies will be mastered.

Section Two Summary: Issues Unique to Implementing CBE in Higher Education

CBE emphasizes mastery of higher order knowledge, skills and attitudes (as defined by The Taxonomy) and the importance of teaching the transfer of academic skills to the workplace. The defining characteristic of CBE can serve colleges and universities well as they work to accommodate the demand for broadly educated and well trained professionals for the 21st Century. The emphasis on the transferability of knowledge, skills and attitudes does not limit CBE to training applications. Higher education has always been concerned with the transferability of skills. The difference is whether this transfer is viewed as easy and automatic or, itself, an acquired skill.

CBE as applied to higher education is a positive response to the claim that higher education is about more than training, if training is taken to mean "doing by rote". By emphasizing the link between instruction and transfer of knowledge and skills, the importance of active learning and the role of assessment, CBE challenges the over reliance on lecture method characteristic of most college classrooms. Lecturing highlights what the teacher is doing; active learning strategies highlight what the student is doing. Knowledge based learning assumes that the student will transfer knowledge into insight, application, analysis, synthesis and evaluation skills that will enhance the student's job performance in the future. CBE makes no such assumption. CBE insists that mastery of the transfer of academic skills to the workplace needs to be part of the instructional process. In short, Competency Based Education does not challenge the values of higher order thinking in higher education. CBE challenges the way in which traditional methods of education have sought to develop these abilities in students.

Conclusion

Some in higher education fear that Competency Based Education represents the abandonment of the best traditions of higher education. By reframing the issue in terms of the need to specify the goals of higher education in operational terms, link instructional strategies directly to those goals and focus assessment on the patterns of evidence that indicate attainment of those goals, CBE actually provides a tool for safeguarding those traditions from an uncritical preparation for professional engagement. In this view, far from being an enemy of higher education, CBE is a tool for linking the best of what we have been doing with the challenge to do better. Increasingly, small colleges and universities must improve their ability to meet the needs of at-risk students and strengthen their mastery of higher levels of academic achievement. Competency Based Education *does not* dictate curriculum. It does focus attention on the importance of college level learning that is not dominated by knowledge-based learning, the role of instruction that teaches and assesses the transfer of academic skills into non-academic settings, and the importance of both formative and summative assessment. Competency Based Education does not rely on or dictate one teaching methodology. Competency Based Education is critical of any method that assumes information in-put/behavior output as the learning process. CBE assumes as do most experienced higher education professionals that the primary goal of the undergraduate experience is to teach students how to get information and what to do with it when they get it.

Traditional approaches to higher education have always insisted that college level learning must involve more than rote memorization. Competency Based Education provides a framework for instructional design, the development of pedagogical tools and an approach to assessment that allows that goal to be achieved with greater precision and more accountability. As more attention is given to the implications of CBE for the higher education setting several issues need further discussion. Among these are: the inter-relationship between the three

120

levels of the taxonomy; the implications of other learning theories for understanding CBE; new models for integrated learning; the design and use of effective formative and summative assessment tools, and, perhaps the largest of all issues, the logistical implications of delivering Competency Based Education to diverse student populations.

Students who enter college well prepared for higher education are less dependent on clearly stated objectives, carefully designed instructional environments and assessment tools than those will less academic readiness. This may be due to the fact that these better prepared students come to college from high schools in which the principles of Competency Based Education describe those secondary programs. Whatever the reason, those well -prepared students are not representative of all students being served by institutions of higher education. They are especially not representative of colleges and universities serving the urban poor.

Small church affiliated institutions of higher education commonly share an intense commitment to link the resources of higher education to the needs of the communities they serve. That mission is woven into the spiritual and academic makeup of the institution. Competency Based Education allows these institutions to meet the needs of a student population that has diverse levels of academic readiness. While CBE is not the only element in the institutions response to the needs of the community it serves it is the key element of the academic program. CBE allows the college to cast a net that is wider than reliance on prior academic experience for successful completion of the college degree. CBE enhances the ability of the college to create pathways to success for those who might otherwise get left behind in two critical ways. First, CBE has transforming potential. That is, it can increase the likelihood that academic programs will not only prepare students to enter professions but also give leadership to their communities and professions by preparing students for the existing and evolving demands of professional life in the 21st century. The transforming potential of CBE prepares students, especially graduate students, to a) contribute to reformulating the consensus of competencies of their professional organizations in the future, and b) return to their communities with an educational experience that enables them to use their skills to strengthen and rebuild those communities. Second, CBE can *increase* the likelihood that students will experience *academic success*, a critical component of students' willingness to persist toward degree completion. (fn. Retention and Persistence literature) By incorporating both student-based (formative assessment) and curriculum based (summative assessment) principles to guide teaching, learning and assessment it becomes possible for more students to attain higher levels of learning with greater degrees of competence. This increased probability of success strengthen the link between institutions of higher education and the communities they serve.

Chapter 5

A Competency Based Approach to Teaching Social Justice

In A Human Services Program

Eileen Stenzel

Introduction

A commitment to realizing greater social justice is an integral part of the intended educational outcomes of colleges and universities across the country, especially those that are church-affiliated. This commitment represents an institutional concern to prepare persons to enter professions with an awareness of and an ability to respond to the needs of those who are on the margins of social, political, economic and educational systems, and the health and human services so vital to sustaining any quality of life. Implementing this commitment in educational programs is a daunting task. This chapter will identify several different models of approaching that task and discuss how the competency based approach of the accrediting agencies within the helping professions offers some new directions for this on-going and important effort.

Three Models of Social Justice Education

1. Values Clarification Pedagogy The longest standing systemic effort to incorporate social justice education into post secondary education is associated

124

with values clarification pedagogy.[45] Values clarification is a process by which individuals recognize how their decisions about how to behavior reflect deeply held values that they may or may not be aware of. Additionally, values clarification pedagogy in an educational setting stresses the developmental importance of assisting individuals in recognizing the value system into which they were socialized, examining that system and making conscious choices about what values will guide and direct their personal and professional choices.

Within higher education, values pedagogy has been used to assist students in recognizing that both persons and systems are value bearers. Decisions are made at both the personal and system levels that reflect deeply embedded value systems. Social justice education has employed values clarification strategies to help students develop tools that make it possible to examine how both personal and systemic behavior functions in relation to sustaining the status quo and fostering change for realizing greater justice.

2. Service Education

Values pedagogy is accompanied by service education as another cornerstone in social justice education. In this model, students engage in various forms of on-going community service in the local communities in which their college or university resides or in immersion programs that reach out to geographic areas where poverty rates are especially high and needs for assistance are especially acute. Often, the traditional-age college students who participate in these service projects find themselves encountering the starkest realities of poverty for the first time. The experience of serving in impoverished communities and the opportunity to examine the impact of this experience on the students' own evolving value system, are distinguishing characteristics of many

---

[45] Howard Kirschenbaum, Leland W. Howe and Sidney B. Simmon, *Values Clarification* (New York: Warner Books, 1995).

The development of social justice competencies is acknowledged as an outgrowth of the focus given to the importance of multicultural competencies within the helping professions.[49] Social justice competencies generally refer to the ability to: a) critically examine social identity as it is shaped by race, ethnicity, gender, sexual orientation, age, class, ability status, religion and national origin; b) critically reflect on how socio-cultural beliefs, assumptions and value systems affect one's approach to the helping process; and c) develop an understanding of and effectiveness in using intervention strategies with persons and groups who represent a broad cross-section of the population. Helping professionals work to identify how an oppressive social and economic environment contributes to and may be at the root of an individual's emotional and behavioral problems. Systemic analysis of dynamics of social injustice not only functions to help the service provider develop a more accurate empathic understanding of the client but also helps the client develop a more accurate picture of him/herself and the challenges he/she is facing.

The American Counseling Association (ACA) now refers to social justice counseling as a "fifth force" in mental health counseling. By this the organization is suggesting that social justice counseling is following psychodynamic, humanistic, behavioral and multicultural approaches to counseling as a driving force in the counseling profession.[50] Social justice counseling incorporates awareness of the cultural context of human behavior to an assessment of the impact that social, political and economic oppression has on psychological well-being. To support this effort, ACA has created a new division within the

---

[49] Nancy Arthur, "Social Justice Competencies for Career Development," The National Consultation on Career Development NATCON 2005, Google, 29 October 2005 <http://www.natcon.org/natcon/papers/natcon_papers_2005_e4.pdf>.

[50] Cf. Manivong Ratts, Michael D'Andrea and Patricia Arredondo, "Social Justice Counseling: 'fifth force' in field," American Counseling Association 2002,1 September 2005 <http://www.counseling.org/Content/NavigationMenu/PUBLICATIONS/COUNSELINGTODAYONLINE/JULY2004/SocialJusticeCounsel.htm>.

128

organization called, "Counselors for Social Justice (CSJ). CSJ mission is to promote social justice initiatives within the various clinical work settings in which counseling service are provided as well as counselor education programs. One of the first tasks of CSJ was to identify the specific competencies one needs to master in order to be effective in social justice counseling and ensuring that these competencies are integrated into counselor education programs. In 2003, the governing board of ACA approved the recommended "Advocacy Competencies" and presented them at the annual ACA meeting.[51]

This effort to expand awareness of how a commitment to social justice impacts mental health services challenges clinical educators to incorporate the development of "Advocacy Competencies" in clinical education programs. The cumulative impact of multicultural competency and social justice competency is that it expands the discussion of social justice education in a higher education to include not only a focus on personal attitudes and values but also on competence, i.e. on identifying and developing the knowledge and skills one needs to engage in the complicated and difficult social, political, economic and cultural issues that define any social justice agenda.

The specificity given to social justice competencies within the various professional organizations that govern the helping professions offers new direction to undergraduate professional education that genuinely strives to prepare the next generation of professionals to be able to engage in the challenges of their chosen profession in a manner that goes beyond being a charitable professional, i.e. one who donates time and money to the less fortunate, or the kind professional, i.e. one who attempts to moderate disparities between organizational culture and social justice concerns through extraordinary efforts. Educational institutions that strive to produce 21st Century Professionals can, in a competency

---

[51] American Counseling Association, 2002, Google, 1 October 2005: <http://www.counseling.org/AM/Template.cfm?Section=RESOURCES>.

based approach to the design and delivery of those programs, produce professional for whom commitments to social justice become part of the ordinary fabric or the profession, of those who work in it and of the relationship that develops between that profession and the communities in which that profession functions.

What does this lofty vision really mean? When social justice becomes identified as a defining characteristic of a profession and a required professional competency it is not longer viewed as the actions of charitable people doing extraordinary things. Rather, social justice is now seen as a desired outcome of professional activity. It is a job requirement. Social justice becomes an integral part of professional identify and competency in achieving greater social justice through how one performs one's job and how a profession functions in the broader social system is the norm, not the exception. It is defining characteristic of the profession, itself, not just some people in that profession. This means that health care providers must be prepared to engage the issue of health care as a social justice issue. This means that business and management professionals must engage personnel and management policy issues as issues of social justice. Law enforcement personnel must engage issues of social justice as part of their professional preparation and performance review. Educators must be prepared to identify how teaching is best done issues related to the need for and attainment of educational outcomes are seen as social justice issues. Civic leaders at all levels will embody a professional identity and standards of practice in which the challenges of managing local, state and national systems of government recognize social justice issues as an integral part of those challenges.

Guided by the work of the various professional associations within the helping professions, educational programs can begin to design learning outcomes, instructional activities and assessment strategies that engage students in the mastery of the knowledge, skill and attitudes sets identified as essential to effective in not only developing a personal commitment to social justice but, as well, using professional skills to realize greater social justice.

Conclusion

A competency based approach to teaching social justice challenges educational institutions to recognize that social justice is not a known entity that can be easily taught. Raising students' awareness of the realities of social and economic inequities, often a defining and important characteristic of service learning programs especially for very advantaged students in higher education, is one thing. Getting to the causes of those inequities is another. Social Justice Education needs to do both to be effective.

Students who have grown up with advantages characteristic of a very small percentage of the world's population need opportunities to experience first hand the broader and starker consequences of the realities of social injustice. They are also a small percentage of the adults enrolled in institutions of higher education, many of whom are far more representative of the population least served by the status quo. Educators need to equip all of these students with what they will need in the real world of economic, political, social and interpersonal reality, to sustain a commitment to social justice that often requires a willingness to preach less and engage more in a messy, difficult, challenging, often contentious and always rich process of engagement with those things that make up the heart and soul of our human experience in any given time and place. Social justice is more than an idea to be embrace. It strives toward action to be taken on behalf of those least served by the way things are.

The educational standards articulated within the various helping professions offer a resource for conceptualizing social justice in terms of the competencies one needs to engage these challenging issues as well as pedagogical strategies for helping students develop those competencies. From the perspective of the helping professions, a commitment to social justice is not an element of the curriculum. Rather it is a requirement of the profession that must be reflected in and developed by the student's entire educational experience.

The notion that each of us harbors a capacity for nobility that co-exists with an equally strong penchant for betrayal, self-promotion, deception and abuse serves as the foundation assumptions about human nature within the human services professions. Life is lived in the tension of our best and worst capacities. The attraction of the profession does not rest in any great mystery about human experience. Rather, it rests in the messiness of human experience that underscores the importance of an approach to social justice education that embraces all elements of efforts to teach social justice in higher education. A competency based approach to social justice education will focus on personal values, develop students' ability to analyze systems, immerse students in the realities of social injustice and the experiences of those among us who suffer the most from it, provide opportunities for student to critically reflect on those experiences, and learn how to advocate and intervene with and on behalf of those who are forced to endure it.

Students fortunate enough to experience a comprehensive, competency based approach to social justice education will, of necessity have to learn how to overcome fear of conflict and give up the need for certainty. They will need opportunities to learn how to value, even revere, the reality of human conflict without assuming that war is the inevitable outcome. They will be challenged to engage with the "stuff of life" that shapes the extent to which any of us truly lives out a commitment to justice at any level. Entering the social justice arena armed with answers, leads one inevitably to wonder what questions were asked, whose experience was listened to and whose interests are being served? The helping professions are a major resource in helping the most creative and energetic higher education professionals further this core component of higher education's contract with humanity.

Conclusion

Barbara Goodman, Darren Henderson, Eileen Stenzel

Accrediting agencies have and will continue to focus attention on the degree to which institutions of higher education are able to demonstrate that their graduates achieve the stated goals of their institution's curriculum. Competency Based Education has emerged as an effective strategy in increasing academic accountability because of its integrated approach to the development of outcomes, the design of instruction and assessment strategies. The debate about its appropriateness for higher education has been framed in terms of process vs. outcomes and education vs. training. In this book, we have tried to show that while that debate leads to some rich discussion, it is, on both counts, based on false assumptions.

Professors in college or university classrooms have and will always work toward implied or explicit outcomes. Where the primary method of instruction is lecturing and the most common assessment tools are a mid-term, a final and a paper, there are still desired outcomes. Those assessments are graded on the degree to which they demonstrate the students' attainment of those outcomes. The assumptions of that methodology are that information in-put will produce those outcomes and that students' native ability or readiness for college-level learning will determine the quality or degree of attainment of the outcomes. Similarly, in college or university classrooms where very specific attention is given to specifying desired outcomes and designing instruction and assessment activities aimed at maximizing attainment of those outcomes, the assumption is that instruction, not just assessment, needs to include teaching students how to learn and opportunities to engage in higher levels of learning. In both models, outcomes and the processes used to achieve them are inextricably linked.

Competency Based Education did not invent the idea of educational attainment, desired outcomes and instructional processes designed to help students achieve them. What it does do, in our experience with it, is offer a language and a structure in which to shape what is essentially a communication process. Competency Based Education provides tools and procedures that make it possible to make implied outcomes explicit, communicate those desired outcomes at the outset to students thereby increasing their ability to engage more actively in the attainment of those outcomes. Regardless of the course of study one pursues, the college experience is for most who experience it, characterized by the challenge to move from ideas and perspectives shaped by the expectations of others, to ideas and perspectives shaped by deep and serious engagement with different and often conflicting points of view. This book has suggested that competency based education done well is as relevant and helpful to that enterprise as it is to the training aspects of the experience of higher education.

Our commitment is not to competency based education. Our commitment is to the integration of process and outcomes as endemic to the teaching-learning process, not something added on to it. Competency based education offers a process of instructional design that has helped us further that effort. An educator designs instruction toward attainment of specific outcomes in order to be able to fully engage in the teaching-learning moment that is every interaction between teacher and student. It is the focused intensity of this engagement that enables a teaching-learning process to occur, movement toward outcomes to be monitored and the emergence of unintended outcomes to be celebrated.

It is our hope that we have been able to offer an alternative to the assumed adverse relationship between education and training, something we see as a false debate that absorbs valuable time and energy. Higher education is and should always be about more than training. Engagement with human history and culture in its multifaceted forms, engagement with the history and culture of the professions and the challenge to go beyond the more homogenous experiences and perspectives of the world in which one is raised go to the heart of what it means to be an educated person. No one who enters the experience of higher education should leave it unmoved, unshaken, unamused, unenlightened or undaunted by all they have yet to see and experience. Higher education is and always has been about more than learning tolerance, as if recognizing the right of another person or idea or point of view to exist is a lofty goal. Tolerance, the notion that such a right is "conferred," simply functions to decrease the violent and abusive acts that intolerance breeds. Higher education is not, in the end, about tolerance, as important as that is. It is about respect for and engagement with the rich landscape of human history and ideas and culture. It is about forays into the fabric of human experience as expressed in imagination, oratory, science, creativity, generosity, corruption, violence, despair, hope, and grand social experiments. Institutions of higher education carry the lion's share of realizing this lofty goal.

Just as important, institutions of higher education prepares the next generation of professionals from doctors, nurses, lawyers, educators, managers, ministers, social workers, counselors, technology specialists of all types, bankers, politicians, economists, artists, and performers to name but a few who will shape the public landscape for decades to come. The degree to which that professional preparation occurs within the broader challenges of the liberal arts may well be the single most important decision higher education makes in the 21st Century. *The Zen of CBE* expresses our experience that successful engagement in the broader liberal arts agenda requires more attention to training in the skills to the learning task than currently is taking place and professional education requires more attention to the importance of critical, comparative engagement than is currently taking place.

This book has really articulated a philosophy of higher education from a multidisciplinary perspective. It sets down some basic, shared principles from which one can proceed. These are: 1) outcomes cannot be separated from the process used to achieve them; 2) the teaching-learning process is one of intense communication that requires a high level of engagement with what the learner is experiencing in the process; 3) the purpose of preparation of instruction is to enable focused engagement and receptivity to the surprises that good teaching and learning always entails, and 4) educators do more than impart information: we teach students how to become more effective learners, especially at the undergraduate level. Working toward desired outcomes creates the parameters that enable the unintended outcomes to be most welcome.

Competency Based Education is not the answer to the challenges encountered in higher education. That resource will always be the dedication and skill of those who choose to devote themselves to this profession. Competency Based Education is a resource for engagement. Its underlying premise is that learning outcomes need to be known and communicated in order to be achieved well. This book expresses our experience with how this communication must reflect an intense, here and now focus on what is taking place in the interaction between student and teacher, on how students are manifesting evidence of attainment of those desired outcomes and, on what adjustments in the moment can take place to broaden and deepen that process.

Far from being a step-by-step manual of instruction, Competency Based Education is more like a magnifying glass for instruction. It holds before us the dual mirrors of progress: the need to know where it is you want to go and the need to know where you are in order to get there.

Bibliography

Åkerlind, Gerlese S. "A New Dimension to Understanding University Teaching."
 Teaching in Higher Education 9 (2004): 363.
American Counseling Association. Google. 1 October 2005.
 <http://www.counseling.org>.
Andrade, Heidi Goodrich. "Teaching with Rubrics." *College Teaching* 53:1
 (2005): 27+. ERIC. EBSCO. Calumet College of St. Joseph, Specker
 Library. 26 July 2005.
Angelo, Thomas A. "Doing Assessment As If Learning Matters Most." *American
 Association for Higher Education Bulletin* 30 May 1999. Academic
 Premier Search. EBSCO. Calumet College of St. Joseph, Specker Library.
 30 May 2003. <http://frontpage.uwsuper.edu/scholars/assess.pdf>
Angelo, Thomas A. and Patricia K. Cross. *Classroom Assessment Techniques.*
 San Francisco: Jossey-Bass, 1993.
"Appendix E: Certifiers of Student Competencies." *Ensuring Quality and
 Productivity in Higher Education* 153 ASHE-ERIC Higher Education
 Report 29.1 (2002): 147-153. Academic Premier Search. EBSCO.
 Calumet College of St. Joseph, Specker Library. 6 July 2005.
Arthur, Nancy. "Social Justice Competencies for Career Development
 Practitioners." *The National Consultation on Career Development*
 NATCON Papers 2005. Google. 29 October 2005.
 <http://www.natcon.org/ catcon/ papers/ natcon_papers_2005e4.pdf>.
Association for Computing Machinery (ACM). "ACM Curricula
 Recommendations." ACM: The First Society of Computing. 2005.
 Google. 1 October 2005. <http://www.acm.org/education/curricula.html>.
The Association for Peace and Justice Studies. Google. 3 October 2005.
 <http://www.peacejusticestudied.org/documents/summer2001.pdf>.
Barthes, Roland. *The Pleasure of the Text.* Trans. Richard Miller. New York: Hill
 and Wang, 1975.
Bloom, Benjamin S. and John Thomas Hastings. *Handbook on Formative and
 Summative Evaluation of Student Learning.* New York, McGraw-Hill,
 1971.
Bloom, Benjamin S., ed. *Taxonomy of Educational Objectives. Handbook I:
 Cognitive Domain.* New York: McKay, 1956.
---. *Taxonomy of Educational Objectives. Handbook II: Affective Domain.* New
 York: McKay, 1973.

Booth, Wayne C., "The Aims of Education." *The Aims of Education.* Chicago: U of Chicago P, 1997.

Bowden, John A. "Competency Based Education—Neither a Panacea Nor a Pariah." Google. 31 July 2002.
<http://crm.hct.ac.ae/events/archive/tend/018bowden.html>.

Brady, L. "Outcome Based Education: Resurrecting the Objectives Debate." *New Education* 16.2 (1994): 69-75.

Bullough, Robert V., Jr., Robert S. Patterson and Clifford T. Mayes. "Teaching as Prophecy." *Curriculum Inquiry* 32:3 (2002): 311-329. Academic Search Premier. EBSCO. Calumet College of St. Joseph, Specker Library. 6 July 2005.

Carneson, John Delpierre and Ken Masters Georges. "Designing and Managing Multiple Choice Questions." The University of of Cape Town South Africa. 1996. Google. 6 July 2005.
<http://www.uct.ac.za/projects/cbe/mcqman/mcqappc.html>.

Chappell, C. "Quality and Competency Based Education and Training." *Literacy Equation.* Red Hill, Australia: Queensland Council for Adult Literacy, 1996.

"Educational Policy and Accreditation Standards." The Council of Social Work Education. Google. 1 November 2005. <http://www.cswe.org/>.

Egan, Gerard. *Exercises in Helping Skills.* California: Brooks/Cole, 1998.

---. *The Skilled Helper.* California: Brooks/Cole, 1998.

"Ethical Standard of Human Services Professional." Statement 16. National Organization of Human Services. Google. 19 September 2005.
<http://www.nohse.com/ethics.html>.

Evers, Frederick T., James C. Rush, and Iris Berdow. *The Bases of Competence: Skills for Lifelong Learning and Employability.* San Francisco: Jossey-Bass, 1998.

Federman, Joel. "Why is Diversity Education Important?" *COPRED Peace Chronicle* 25.4 (2002): 9-10. Google. 19 September 2005.
<http://www.peacejusticestudies.org/documents/summer2001.pdf>.

Fisher, Kath. "Demystifying Critical Reflection: Defining criteria for assessment." *Higher Education Research and Development* November 2003: 315-325. Academic Search Premier. EBSCO. Calumet College of St. Joseph, Specker Library. 10 August 2005.

Fontana, David. *Discovering Zen A Practical Guide to Personal Security.* San Francisco: Chronicle Books, 2001.

Gagne, Robert. *The Conditions of Learning.* New York: Holt, Rinehart and Winston, 1985.

Gardiner, Lion F. *Redesigning Higher Education: Producing Dramatic Gains in Student Learning.* ASHE-ERIC High Education Report 7. Washington D.C.: Graduate School of Education and Human Development, George Washington U, 1994.

Gerald, Green, et. al. *A Critical Analysis of Competency-Based Reforms in Higher Education*. San Francisco: Jossey-Bass, 1979.

Gertler, J., S. Reinach and G. Kuehn. "Non-accident release of Hazmat from railroad Tank Cars: Training Issues." N.p.: Federal Railroad Administration Office of Research and Development, 1999.

Gonczi, Andrew. "Reconceptualizing Competency Based Education and Training: With Particular Reference to Education for Occupations in Australia." August 1996. Google. 6 July 2005. <http://adt.lib.uts.edu.au.uplaods/approved/adt-NTSM20040825.181458/public/02wholelinkingessay.pdf>.

Grant, Gerald, et al. *On Competence: A Critical Analysis of Competency-Based Reforms in Higher Education*. San Francisco: Jossey-Bass, 1979.

Grossman, Robert W. "Encouraging Critical Thinking Using the Case Study Method and Cooperative Learning Techniques." *Electronic Journal on Excellence in Teaching* 5.1 (1994): 7-20. Google. 30 May 2005. <http://ject.lib.muohio.edu/sample/article.php?aticle+57>.

Habanek, Darlene V., "An Examination of the Integrity of the Syllabus." *College Teaching* 53. 2 (2005): 62-65. ERIC. EBSCO. Calumet College of St. Joseph, Specker Library. 26 July 2005.

Harden, R.M. "Developments in outcome-based education." *Medical Teacher* 24.2 (2003): 117-120. ERIC. EBSCO. Calumet College of St. Joseph, Specker Library. 26 July 2005.

Harris, Howard S. and David Maloney, eds. *Human Services*. Boston: Allyn and Bacon, 1999.

Hoogveld, Albert W.M., Fred Paas, and William M.G. Jochems. "Training Higher Education teachers for Instructional Design of Competency-Based Education: Product Oriented Versus Process-Oriented Worked Examples." *Teaching and Teacher Education* 21.3 (2005): 287-297. Abstract. Academic Search Premier. EBSCO. Calumet College of St. Joseph, Specker Library. 5 November 2005. <http://search.epnet.com/login.aspx>.

Hyland, T. *Competence, Education and NVQs: Dissenting Perspectives*. London: Cassell, 1994.

Ianozzi, Maria. "Babson College. Policy Perspectives. Exemplars." Pew Higher Education Roundtable. Philadelphia: Institute for Research on Higher Education, 1998. ERIC. EBSCO. Calumet College of St. Joseph, Specker Library. 1 August 2005.

Jaeger, Audrey J., "Job Competencies and the Curriculum: An Inquiry into Emotional Intelligence into Graduate Professional Education." *Research in Higher Education* 44.6 (2003). ERIC. EBSCO. Calumet College of St. Joseph, Specker Library. 2 September 2005.

Jarvis, P. and S. Parker. "Editorial Competencies for everything?" *International Journal of Lifelong Education* March-April 2004: 123-124. Academic

Search Premier. EBSCO. Calumet College of St. Joseph, Specker Library. 1 August 2005.

Jones, Elizabeth A., Richard A. Voorhees and Karen Paulson. "Defining and Assessing Learning: Exploring Competency-Based Initiatives." *Report of the National Postsecondary Education Cooperative Working Group on Competency-Based Initiatives in Postsecondary Education.* Washington D.C.: U.S. Department of Education, 2002.

Jenkins, Alan and Dave Unwin. "How to write learning outcomes." Writing learning outcomes for the Core Curriculum. NCGIA GISCC Learning Outcomes. 27 June 1996. 29 March 2001 <http: www.Ncgia.ucsb.edu/education/curricula/ giscc/units/format/outcomes.html>.

Kass, Leon R., "The Aims of Liberal Education." *The Aims of Education.* Chicago: U of Chicago P, 1997.

Kerka, Sandra. "Competency-Based Education and Training: Myths and Realities." Clearing House on Adult, Career and Vocational Education (ACVE). 1998. ERIC. EBSCO. Calumet College of St. Joseph, Specker Library. 2 September 2005.
<http://www.cete.org/acve/textonly/docgen.asp>.

Kirschenbaum, Howard, Leland W. Howe, and Sidney B. Simmon, eds. *Values Clarification.* New York: Warner Books, 1995.

Klausmeier, H.J. *Educational Psychology.* New York: Harper and Row, 1985.

Krathwohl, David, Benjamin S. Bloom and Bertram B. Masia. *Taxonomy of Educational Objectives The Classification of Educational Goals Handbook I: The Cognitive Domain.* New York: McKay, 1954.

---. *Taxonomy of Educational Objectives The Classification of Education Goals Handbook II: Affective Domain.* New York: McKay, 1956.

Kuehn, George. Personal Interview. 15 July 2000.

Morarji, Karuna. "The Continuing Relevance of Gandhi's Views on Education in India and Beyond." *COPRED Peace Chronicle* 25.4 (2001): 1, 10-13. The Association for Peace and Justice Studies. Google. 3 October 2005. <http://www.peacejusticestudied.org/documents/summer2001.pdf>.

Palomba, Catherine A. and Trudy W. Banta. *Assessment Essentials.* San Francisco: Jossey-Bass, 1999.

Pisirg, Robert M. *Zen and the Art of Motorcycle Maintenance.* Toronto: Bantam Books, 1984.

Proctor, Robert E. *Defining the Humanities: How Rediscovering a Tradition Can Improve our Schools.* Bloomington: Indiana UP, 1998.

Ratts, Manivong, Michael D'Andrea and Patricia Arredondo. "Social Justice Counseling: 'fifth force' in the Field." The American Counseling Association. 2002. Google. 2 September 2005.
<http://www.counseling.org/Content/NavigationMenu/

PUBLICATIONS/COUNSELINGTODAYONLINE/JULY2004/SocialJus
ticeCounsel.htm>.

Riccardi, Joseph N. "Achieving Human Services Outcomes Through
Competency-Based Training: A Guide for Managers." *Behavior
Modification* 29.3 (2005): 488-507. ERIC. EBSCO. Calumet College of
St. Joseph, Specker Library. 6 July 2005.

Smith, Mark. "Competence and Competency." Infed. January 2005. Google. 18
May 2005. <http://www.infed.org/biblio/b-comp.htm>.

Stables, Andrew. "From Discrimination to Deconstruction: four modulations of
criticality in the humanities and social sciences." *Assessment & Evaluation
in Higher Education* December 2003: 665-672. ERIC. EBSCOHOST.
Calumet College of St. Joseph, Specker Library. August 2005.

"Statement on Multicultural Competencies." The American Counseling
Association. Google. 1 October 2005. <http://www.
Counseling.org/Content/Navigation/Menu?RESOURCES
MULTICULTURALANDDIVERSITYISSUES/Multicultural_and_D.htm
>.

*Suggestions for Effective Railroad Tank Car Loading/Unloading Training
Programs: Instructional Methods.* N.p.: Publication of Federal Railroad
Administration Office of Research and Development, 1999. Google. 1
July 2000. <http://www.fra.dot.gov/downloads/safety/sertcl2.pdf>.

Sullivan, Rick. "The Competency-Based Approach to Training." The RePro Line
The Reading Room. JHPIEGO Strategy Paper. September 1995. Google. 6
July 2005.
<http://www.reproline.jhu.edu/english/6read/6training/cbt/cbt.htm#CBT>.

Tate, Allen. *Four Essays of Four Decades.* Chicago: Swallow Press, 1968.

Tomasa, Lynne. "Strategy to Implement Competency-Based Education."
ACGME Outcomes Project Educational Outcomes Group. Google. 1
September 2005. <http://www. Ahsc.arizona.edu/azmet/
Strategy%20to%20Implement%20Competency%20Based%20Education.p
df>.

Trigwell, Keith and Suzanne Shale. "Student Learning and the Scholarship of
University Teaching." *Studies in Higher Education* 29.4 (2004): 523.

Trivett. David A. *Competency Programs in Higher Education.* ERIC/Higher
Education Research Report 7, 1075. Washington D.C.: American
Association for Higher Education, 1975.

Voorhes, Alice Bedard. "Creating and Implementing Competency-Based
Learning Models." *Measuring What Matters Competency-Based Learning
Models in Higher Education.* Ed. Richard A. Voorhes. New Directions for
Institutional Research 110. San Francisco: Jossey-Bass, 2001.

Waghid, Y. Peters. "Non-instrumental Justification of Higher Education View
Revisited: Contesting the Philosophy of Outcome-based Education in
South Africa." *Studies in Philosophy and Education* 22.3/4 (2003): 245+.

142

Wang, Xin. "Competency-Based Education." <u>Baylor University</u>. Google. 29 April
     2002. <http://www3.baylor.edu/ Xin_Wang/pdf/competency.pdf>.
Warn, James and Paul Tranter. "Measuring Quality in Higher Education: a
     competency approach." *Quality in Higher Education* 7.3 (2001): 191-198.
Weinrach, Steven G. and Kenneth R. Thomas. "A Critical analysis of the
     Multicultural Counseling Competencies: Implications for the Practice of
     Mental Health Counseling." *Journal of Mental Health Counseling* 24.1
     (2002): 20-35.
<u>Wikipedia, the free encyclopedia</u>. 31 May 2005. 1 August 2005.

Index